Showtime

How to Make Thousands Vacationing in Hawaii

By Art Fettig

*Cover and Special Artwork
by Bill Tatroe*

36 Fairview, Battle Creek, MI 49017
Phone 1-800-441-7676 (616) 965-2229
Fax (616) 965-4522

Manufactured in the United States of America

Design, Layout and Typesetting
by

Library of Congress
Catalog Number 94-77452
Fettig, Art
Showtime

ISBN 0-916927-19-9

Dedication

I would like to dedicate this book to all of the people who shared our adventure and made it possible.

Our thanks to those beautiful children at Sacred Heart Academy for being themselves. The love they share for one another is truly inspiring.

Our thanks to the members of the Hawaiian Chapter of the National Speaker's Association for their warm hospitality.

Thanks to the United States Navy at Pearl Harbor. They made us feel welcome and worthwhile.

To the members of the American Society of Safety Engineers we extend our gratitude.

To everyone who attended the Governor's Pacific Rim Safety and Health Conference we give our heartfelt appreciation.

To Paula Hopkins who manned our office while I trotted with joy so far away, my thanks for making me feel that things were in good hands.

To the people of Hawaii I say *Aloha*, *Mahalo* and God Bless.

And to Terry Pochert, a friend, an associate, a coach and a cheerleader I borrow a line from Bob Hope and say, "Oh thanks for the memory."

Showtime

When I was a kid about eighteen or nineteen years of age I worked in an office in Detroit for Grand Trunk Western Railroad. Once a year the office staff would get together for a special night out. We would drive through the Windsor Tunnel over to Canada to the *Elmwood Casino* and have dinner at the *Ambassador Room.*

The *Ambassador Room* was a high class nightclub and they had a dancing singing chorus, a fine orchestra and they featured either a great comic or a famous singer each week. Every show at the *Ambassador* started with the chorus ladies and they would dance around the stage as they sang the following:

It's Show Time at the Ambassador Room
Show time at the Ambassador Room.
If you're with your sweetheart,
Your mother or dad,
This is where the best time
In the town's to be had...

Then a booming voice would say, "And now ladies and gentlemen, your Master of Ceremonies...." and they'd name the MC of the show.

For some reason that I cannot understand that song popped into my head this morning at 2:30 A.M. I had just awakened and I had an overpowering desire to get out of bed and do some exercises. Exercising tremendous willpower, I overcame this overpowering desire and closed my eyes. That was when the song came into my head. After four more hours of sleep I was ready to face reality. The reality was that I really needed exercise.

It had been a long, long winter. One of the longest, coldest winters we'd had in Michigan in some time. My gas bills attested to the fact that we had experienced more zero and below zero weather in this year, than in many previous years.

The only reason I am mentioning the weather is that I would like to justify the fact that my big fat gut is hanging out over my belt once again. Under many circumstances I can live with a fat gut without alarm. The problem though is that in just three weeks I will not be facing normal circumstances. In three weeks it is *Showtime* for me.

Let me try to explain and to introduce myself. I am Art Fettig and I write books and give speeches for a living. Sometime ago I came to the admission that being a professional speaker is really being in show business.

Standing in front of an audience and making them laugh or cry, and then hopefully, helping them to do their jobs better or safer and doing this for a living is really a form of show business. You might not think of the late Dr. Norman Vincent Peale as having been Mr. Show Business, but please, just go along with me this once. Speaking is a lot like singing or dancing or acting too.

So what does all this have to do with my fat gut? Well, the fact is that in three weeks, yes, it is three weeks, exactly to the day, I will be visiting Honolulu. I have been asked to do a speech for the Governor's Pacific Rim Safety Conference at Honolulu on April 22.

Today is March 28 and so if that were my only concern I would have some twenty-five days to get in shape. The fact is that once I got this invitation I went to work finding other opportunities to speak.

The second booking was for a luncheon for members of the American Society of Safety Engineers on April 19. Next I booked two sessions for the United States Navy at Pearl Harbor for the morning of April 20 and that is where I started thinking about getting into shape. After all, a bunch of able bodied seamen do not want a fat old man telling them about anything.

I compounded the challenge by inviting a man named Terry Pochert to come along on the trip with his video camera. Terry is one of the best cameramen and video producers I have ever met. Better yet, Terry seems to be fascinated with producing video tapes of my performances.

We've worked successfully on a number of projects and when I mentioned Hawaii, Terry immediately said, "Count me in! We will shoot everything you do."

After a few telephone calls and faxes to the U.S. Navy, they said, "Yes." They would love a video series of my talks on safety. After that, Terry and I decided to do some video tapes based on some children's songs I had written. We have some great audio tapes produced by a very creative young man named Paul Lee Marr and we want to shoot some videos of wonderful kids singing our songs.

Hawaii is the perfect place in the whole world to shoot videos of kids because they have the most beautiful children in the world, children of every race and color. Two more faxes and phone calls booked us at *Sacred Heart Academy* in Honolulu where they have promised us kids of every age and every color of the rainbow.

I promised to do some programs for the kids and maybe a teacher's and a parent's program in return for their help. All this was scheduled for Monday, April 18.

After that, someone called and asked if I would speak to the Rotary Club of Honolulu at noon on April 20. We said yes and we will have to go straight from the Navy programs at Pearl Harbor, downtown to a fancy hotel for the Rotary.

Then we topped it all off by promising to do a program at a Pupus for members of the National Speakers Association on Monday after our program with the teachers. A Pupus is a twilight meeting on the beach, with hor d'oeuvres' and cocktails. (Do not ask me what hor d'oeuvres' are.)

"We will shoot it all, every bit of it." Terry said when I told him our schedule.

So, this morning at 2:30 A.M. when I woke up and my body told me I should get up and start exercising it was just a natural thing. My body is a mess. I could recite a list of aches and pains that would fill this whole sheet. Frankly, I must admit that quite likely, all of those problems come from the fact that I have been eating all the wrong foods and avoiding my daily exercise for far too long. Becoming a widower last June 26th, after thirty-eight years of marriage simply did not condition me for my own cooking. Sadly, good nutrition is not high on my list.

As a matter of information let me tell you that I will be sixty-five on July 5 this year. That is an event that I am not really looking forward to. Now with *Showtime* approaching I have made a pact with myself this morning. I plan to walk a minimum of two brisk miles every day until our plane lands in Honolulu on April 16th at 12:32 P.M. on American Airlines. Not only must I be in good physical condition by that time, I must also get my mind in order.

Speaking for that wide a range of audiences is a challenge in itself. I must come up with talks on attitudes, safety, teaching, parenting, some interesting programs for children, a talk on speaking for professional speakers, something for the Rotary and then, hopefully, six or seven different things for the U.S. Navy to create a small video series.

I figure we have nineteen days, counting today, until we fly off to Honolulu. Twenty-one days until our first program with the students at *Sacred Heart Academy.* Then that evening we speak for professional speakers.

If I simply rehearse a bit of speech material each morning when I'm doing my daily walks it will start me out on the right track. Then if I make a file for each program and.... gosh, I've really got my work cut out for me in Honolulu.

Kids, teachers, parents, professional speakers, safety engineers, the U.S. Navy, the Rotary and then a breakfast meeting for attendees at the Governor's Pacific Rim Safety Conference.

I am excited. I am challenged and I am also a bit bushed because you see, I just returned from the mall where I did a really brisk two and a quarter miles. Before that I put on a great Louis Armstrong CD and did a hundred twists, fifty toe touches, fifty good arm swings and I have just begun. I plan to get in the habit of working out about every hour. Nothing elaborate, mind you, just some bends, anything that might help to get this gut of mine smaller and tightened up.

I am committed. I am determined. I have set my sights and I will not falter in my mission. After all, remember, in just twenty-one days, in Hawaii, *It's Showtime.*

Just Say Yes

It is 7:25 A.M. and I am sopping wet. I just did three and a half laps around the mall, briskly. That is about two and a third miles and before I came to the mall I did a good series of exercises accompanied to the wonderful music of Louis Armstrong.

Yesterday was quite productive and I made up files for each of the sessions we have planned in Hawaii. As I walked around the mall I visualized ahead to Monday morning, April 18. Terry and I are surrounded with absolutely beautiful kids and we are shooting pictures of the children singing our song titled *"Just Say Yes."* The lyrics go like this:

JUST SAY YES

Just say "Yes,"	*Just say "Yes,"*	*Just say "Hey there*
To believing you're special	*To trying harder*	*I'm somebody*
Just say "Yes,"	*Just say "Yes,"*	*And you are too*
To being kind	*To hanging in.*	*Let's do our best."*
Just say "Yes,"	*Just say "Yes,"*	*Stand up! Listen*
To caring for others	*To growing daily.*	*To what is right,*
Just say "Yes,"	*Just say "Yes,"*	*Respect yourself*
To improving your mind.	*To learning to win.*	*And just say, "Yes."*

Art Fettig

There is a bit more to this than that. My musician friend Paul Lee Marr added a chorus that goes:

Just say "Yes," when you want to be better
When you want to reach the other side.
Gotta say "Yes."
No doesn't cut it, cause you'll never rise above it.
But just say "Yes," you're really going to love it.

I can see our children, probably aged five to nine or so and we have a big boom box out on the playground.
"Just Say Yes, Just Say Yes."
Talk about visualizing. The third trip around the mall I was already back from Hawaii and Terry had done a fantastic job of editing the *"Just Say Yes Rap"* Kareoke video. Kids all over the world were gathering in front of their television sets in schools singing this song together as the words flashed on the screen.
"Just say yes to believing you're special. Just say yes to being kind." I've written books for children on being special and being kind. In fact, we have an entire, non-threatening value system contained in that *"Just Say Yes"* verse.
Take another look at the verses please. We've developed a little activity book to help teachers teach their students each of the values, one each week.
We have achievement cards to track each student's success too. Our *Three Robot* characters are Pos, the happy successful little girl robot, Semi-Pos, the not-now, maybe tomorrow robot and Neg, the negative robot who brightens up a room just by leaving. *The Three Robots* join forces to share powerful, positive living concepts with the students.
We have been working with our *Three Robots* for so many years and we have reached thousands of students. The problem is that in America today we are raising millions, not thousands, of children who do not seem to have a solid, positive set of values on which to build a successful life.
My dream is to reach millions of students with our *"Just Say Yes"* message. Oh it is fun to visualize. It is well worth the effort and the pain that I am experiencing each morning just getting my aging body in good shape for this Hawaiian trip.

I'm exercising my mind each morning too and my imagination. I'm planning to make my dream come true.

Wouldn't this be a better world if our *Three Robots* could teach every kid to start the day saying "I'm happy! I'm healthy! I'm somebody! And you're somebody too!

Sure it would and that is what I'm working for every day, making this a better world for all of our children.

Moving Faster

Yesterday the folders on my talks got a bit thicker. I laid out the whole talk for the Honolulu Rotary Club. It should be inspirational, entertaining, humorous and yet challenging.

I did a lot of work on my talks for the Navy. I will tell you more about that presentation as I get it in order. I know what thirty-two to forty minutes of that talk will be, but I am facing a lot of decisions on the other eighty minutes of presentation time they have promised me.

We will be endeavoring to create a whole series of videos, the one about thirty-two minutes and then a whole series of short videos that we call meeting sizzlers. These should run about ten minutes each so if things go tremendously well we might complete six or seven or even eight tapes.

This morning I walked up a good sweat. I am here at the mall now cooling down and reviewing the speech material I was rehearsing as I made my walk.

Today I was working on a verse I had written several years ago for teachers. I used to do it from memory, but since I haven't done it a lot lately I must brush up on it. It has nine stanzas and goes as follows:

Teacher, Teacher

Teacher, Teacher
help me learn
when to press on
when to turn.

Teacher, Teacher
help me grow
hug me, I need
hugging so.

Teacher, Teacher
give me hope
won't you show me
how to cope.

Teacher, Teacher
guide my way,
teach me what
I ought to say.

Teacher, Teacher
I'm worthwhile
won't you give me
just one smile?

Teacher, Teacher
you're so grand,
when you help
me understand.

Teacher, Teacher
light a spark,
help me see it
through the dark.

Teacher, Teacher
when you care
you prove love's
a thing we share.

Teacher, Teacher
yes it's true,
Teacher, Teacher
We love you.

Somewhere recently I read that today, time is more valuable to people than money. Everything seems to be moving faster. People's attention span seems to be shrinking.

I repeated the *Teacher* poem again and again as I walked and there were a couple of stanzas that bothered me. I think the most powerful line is the one that says, "Teacher, Teacher, help me grow. Hug me, I need hugging so." It might be powerful but it is also dangerous in today's world. In many or most schools today, teachers are no longer allowed to hug their students.

I think that is tragic. I have read a number of reports that show hugs are good for you in many, many ways and some kids come into school without a hug in their life.

Sure, there are problems. Sure, there are child molesters. Sure, we want to protect our children but just the same, hugging is not something I would prohibit.

Just the same, change is change and so this morning I decided to cut the verse from nine to six stanzas and hugging was out. I dropped that hope-cope line too.

You might not believe what I am about to tell you now. The line that goes, "Teacher, Teacher, light a spark, help me see it through the dark." is being dropped because too many fifth graders think that the line is sexual in nature.

Evidently many fifth grade students have been exposed to such a daily bombardment of sexual innuendo on television that they can find double meanings everywhere. The line is out. We have cut the verse 33 1/3 percent.

An old Woody Guthrie song goes, "The times they are a changing." The fact is that I must keep on moving faster and faster every day now, just to remain where I am at.

Empathy

Sopping wet. That's what I am this morning. Sopping wet, and I feel good all over. I did four brisk laps around the mall and then just enough more to make it a total of three miles.

If I hope to be in shape for that schedule we've set for ourselves in Hawaii then I think it is important that I go all out on these laps this morning. I am up to thirty sit-ups, twice a day and more bends and toe touches.

I am doing facial exercises too. I have noticed this sag in my double chin and I am determined to tighten that up by the time I face those cameras. One exercise is sort of doing chin-ups. I pull up hard on my chin. Another is to do broad smile exercises. I do a hundred of each as I walk around the mall. I try to do these in private but that is not easy in such a public place.

Then I do my eye rises. I have a tendency to squint and I believe that a hundred daily wide eye stretches just might help.

This morning I was thinking about those videos we will be doing for the Navy. One of those ten minute videos we will be doing is to stress the importance of empathy. I recite the following poem titled *The Builder* written by Jess Kenner.

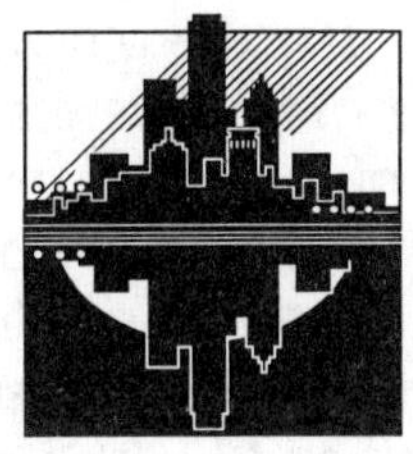

The Builder

I watched them tearing a building down-
A gang of men in a busy town,
With ho-heave-ho and lusty yell
They swung a beam and a side wall fell;
I asked the foreman, "Are these men skilled
and the men you'd hire if you had to build?"

He gave a laugh and said, "No, indeed.
Just common labor is all I need;
I can easily wreck in a day or two
what builders have taken a year to do!"
And I thought to myself as I went away
"Which of these roles have I tried to play?"

Am I a builder who works with care, measuring
life by the rule and square?
Am I shaping my deed to well made plan,
patiently doing the best I can?
Or am I a wrecker, who walks the town,
Content with the labor of tearing down.

By Jess Kenner

When I do this poem for an audience it doesn't quite go that way though. When I get half way through the poem I find I am pathetically lost. I stutter. I stammer. I grope. I try to start up again and again without success. It seems that all of my energy is draining out of my body and my whole presentation is disintegrating.

After a horrible silence I finally ask, "How many of you think that the old whiz kid really messed up?" Next I ask, "How many of you were saying, Gosh, I'm glad that isn't me making a fool of myself?"

How many of you were sitting there saying, "Man, I wish I knew that next line? I wish I could get you started again, because I know just how you feel. I have been there before myself and I wish I could help you."

Well, I am not going to burden you, the reader, with this whole thing that I was rehearsing on my walk this morning. Let me just say that what I share with the audience is that one of the keys to greatness is the ability to walk in another person's shoes. That when we can feel true empathy for another that we really begin to grow as a human being.

So this morning I practiced that poem again and again. I practiced getting lost and then I practiced my recovery. At the end of the ten minute video I recite *The Builder* with everything I have in me.

There is drama and passion and eloquence. It is what I do and if I do it right then it is a piece of material that will stick to their mind.

Hopefully it will touch someone's heart too and they will be caught up in the spirit of empathy. Oh, the walls of prejudices we could eliminate if we could only learn to see situations from the other person's point of view.

Well, I have cooled down now and it is time to get on with the rest of my life.

Love Is Quite Different

There they go again, those pictures in my mind. I did all my facial exercises and even my prayers on the first lap and I was half way around the second lap when those pictures started flashing in my mind.

It is Monday morning, April 18, and I am sitting down surrounded by a dozen or two dozen absolutely beautiful Hawaiian kids. They are sitting on the ground in a sort of semi-circle and I am telling them about a scene from the movie *South Pacific*.

Emile DeBecque, the French planter, was talking with Marine Lieutenant Joseph Cable, about prejudice. DeBecque had fallen in love with Ensign Nellie Furbush and Lieutenant Cable had fallen for Bloody Mary's daughter, Liat. The Lieutenant sang a song with the following words:

You've Got To Be Carefully Taught

You've got to be taught to hate and fear.
You've got to be taught from year to year.
It's got to be drummed in your dear little ear-
You've got to be carefully taught.
You've got to be taught to be afraid
Of people whose eyes are oddly made
And people whose skin is a different shade-
You've got to be carefully taught.

> *You've got to be taught before it's too late,*
> *Before you are six or seven or eight,*
> *To hate all the people your relatives hate-*
> *You've got to be carefully taught.*

I have been to the Hawaiian schools and seen those children who seem to come in every color of the rainbow. Black and white and every color in between. They are precious and they seem more loving than any children I have ever met.

Oscar Hammerstein wrote the lyrics for *South Pacific* and Richard Rogers the music. In a book about Oscar Hammerstein I read that he had written a second verse to that song that the Lieutenant had sung.

The author of the book did not know why the second verse had been cut from the play before it opened on Broadway. Perhaps the play ran too long, or maybe Richard Rogers did not like it.

In any event just that one chorus was sung. The words were so shocking and powerful that *South Pacific* was banned in the racially turbulent South.

Here are the words of the second chorus:

> *Love is quite different, it grows by itself.*
> *It will grow like a weed on a mountain of stones,*
> *You don't have to feed it or put fat on its bones;*
>
> *It can live on a smile or a note of a song;*
> *It may starve for a while, but it stumbles along,*
> *Stumbles along with its banners unfurled,*
> *The joy and the beauty, the hope of the world.*

The pictures in my mind show Terry with his camera behind me, shooting a video of those beautiful, loving children who, thank God, have never been taught to hate.

This is the title of a book I wrote on love and I learned a lot of what I know about loving just watching those loving children in Hawaii.

What's It Like?

*T*hat's the idea this morning. What is it like to be a professional speaker for over twenty years? It is one of the themes that the professional speakers of Hawaii want me to talk about at their Pupus on Monday evening, April 18 and so that is what I thought about on my walk.

Today I slept in. It is Saturday and I was up late last night doing research. No excuse to not walk though and so, since the sun was shining and it was a beautiful spring day, I opted to walk outside. I did a full fifty minutes flat out and a lot of thoughts and memories filled my mind as I walked.

What is it like to be a professional speaker? Well, it is much better than any other occupation that I have seen. It is really rewarding at times. I love doing the speeches. I even enjoy doing the research for those talks. The thing I do not like is getting those speeches. That is the back breaker. Getting the bookings to keep you busy and in front of people.

Speaking is pure joy most of the time. People laugh. People cry. People call you and tell you that you changed their lives for the better. They come up to you and thank you for your program as if it is a special gift that you brought them. People give you standing ovations and often they buy all of your books and your tapes and they frequently pay you a fat fee besides.

What is not to like about being a professional speaker when people praise and applaud your work and then thank you from their hearts for doing it? Just maybe it is the best job in the world when it comes to the actual doing of the speech.

Unfortunately, the actual performance is just the tip of a huge iceberg.

I can visualize that audience. Like most meetings of the National Speakers Association, the audience will be made up of a few seasoned veterans and the rest of the audience will be made up of almost speakers and those just really getting started.

They are seeking ways of improving their current income and a few will be seeking ways to improve their speeches and their performance. I guess the real secret to success is to get good at speaking and to get good at letting people know you are alive and available.

What is it like to be a professional speaker for over twenty years? It is good. It is wonderful. It is heartwarming. There are ten great memories for every bad one and the bad one was not that bad if I learned from it.

There are horror stories about transportation and yet I can honestly say that I only missed one booking in all that time and I came awfully close to making that one. I finally made it all the way to Atlanta and was boarded on a little plane for Chattanooga when they canceled the flight at the last moment because of an engine problem.

Fortunately, I had another professional speaker standing by just in case I couldn't make it and things worked out fine. They asked me back later to do the talk for their audience.

I could write a book on the special challenges that come up. Members of the audience having their hearts stop during your talk. Power shortages. A lady whose hair caught on fire because of a short in her hearing aid. Minor disturbances like that. Hecklers, drunks, there is not much they could throw my way that I have not already experienced, and yet every audience is a joy to face for me now.

It is like being especially honored in life to be a professional speaker. That is what it is like. It is an awesome responsibility if you really take your job seriously. Sometimes when you walk out in front of a few thousand people and they stand up and cheer you get a big lump in your throat and think to yourself, "Today I am the luckiest person in the world."

That is what I will tell that audience. I will tell them that it is wonderful, but that it is rough and that, probably, most of them will not make it. So many drop out along the road to success.

Sure, I'm lucky but I've read that luck is when preparation meets opportunity. Believe me, I work on that preparation every day of my life. That is what this book is all about, preparation. I am preparing physically and mentally for every one of those special audiences in Hawaii.

This morning about half way through my walk the perspiration was really flowing and this idea popped into my head that I was really a sort of an athlete in training for a big event, or in this case, a whole list of big events.

Some of those talks might have small audiences but that is not the true measure of things. For me the true measure is this, "Can I touch one life with my talk?" If the answer is yes then that is truly an important audience.

So I believe I will ask that speaker's audience this question, "Are you in this for what you can get or for what you can give?" My answer to them is this. If you are just in it for the getting then you will not make it, but that will be true not just in the speaking profession but in life itself.

You really do have to give to get and to be happy you must learn to give for the joy of giving.

Greatness

*T*oday is Easter Sunday and I went to church early and now I am at the mall. I did a bit over three miles this morning and at home before coming to the mall I managed to do thirty-eight sit-ups, fifty toe touches and an array of the easier twists and turns.

I feel marvelous this morning and I know for certain that I am on the right path. Those love handles on my hips are quickly disappearing and my gut is truly getting smaller.

This morning I visualized myself giving a thirty minute talk for the Honolulu Rotary Club. The talk is scheduled for a noon meeting on Wednesday, April 20 at a fancy Waikiki hotel. The title of my talk is *"Bringing Out That Greatness in Yourself and in Others."*

This morning I was practicing a story about a magnificent sculpture I once saw in Florence, Italy. The story goes that many years ago a famous sculptor was hired to create a masterpiece. They purchased a huge piece of marble over twenty feet high and rather narrow for a sculpture. The artist worked on the piece for a while and then he lost his inspiration and abandoned the project.

The huge piece of marble just lay there for some thirty years and it was sort of an embarrassment to the city because it had cost a great deal of money.

Finally another artist was commissioned to complete the project. The piece of marble was cleaned up and the artist inspected the piece and then with great flair, he announced that he would not work on the project because the piece of marble had a flaw at the base.

Finally the committee in charge approached Michaelangelo. He took one look at the piece of marble and went to work. He toiled with his hammer and chisel for two years, from 1401 to 1403 and finally he was finished.

The committee called in the world's finest critics and after viewing the result, that statue of David, the critics were unanimous in their verdict. This was truly the greatest sculpture ever created. After this pronouncement, someone interviewed Michaelangelo and they asked him how he could create such a masterpiece. His rendering was almost lifelike. People stared at the statue and often swore they could see it breathing.

"It was already there," Michaelangelo explained. "I didn't see that piece of marble at all. I saw David who killed Goliath, David in all his splendor. All I had to do was take my hammer and my chisel and knock away the pieces that did not belong there."

Of course my message for the members of the Honolulu Rotary is this; that every one of us, every one of our children and every one of the people we know are really masterpieces. Some of them still have chips on their shoulders. Some are still in the rough. But each of them and each of us has that potential for greatness.

Our challenge each day is to work on ourselves and to assist each other to come a bit closer to reaching our true potential. That is the message. **There is greatness in you.**

Passion

*I*t's starting our second week today. I feel I am making real progress. For an Easter Sunday I didn't pig out too much. I was sensible all the way both in what I ate and how much. I do believe that my stomach is getting smaller. Not small, but smaller. With a little luck, just maybe, no kid will sneak up on me lying on the beach in Waikiki and paint "blimp" on my belly.

Today I am working on a talk for the safety engineers titled *"Developing a Passion for Safety."* The same talk might be titled, *"Developing a Passion for Anything."* I believe that the real key to passion is the attaining of a level of excellence. It is impossible to develop a passion for something you are really rotten at. When people tell me that they hate their jobs, I want to suggest they try doing their job seeking excellence and to see what happens.

Although Hawaii is really not in the South Pacific, whenever I go there I think about James Michener's book *South Pacific*, the lovely musical with songs by Rogers and Hammerstein. One of the magical moments of the play is when Bloody Mary, a tough, cunning native lady sings *"Happy Talk."* It goes like this:

Happy Talk

Happy talk, keep talkin' happy talk
Talk about somethin' that you'd like to do.
You've got to have a dream
If you don't have a dream
How you goin' to make that dream come true?

Just maybe the reason some people do not move forward is because they are not really going anywhere. Unless you have a destination, how will you know when you have arrived? Unless we set some standard for excellence in our work and in our lives, then it is difficult or impossible to measure our achievements.

Like Bloody Mary said, unless we have a dream, then how are we going to make it come true? How do you develop a passion for anything? You start by setting a simple, achievable goal. You reach one goal, then you set another. You give an effort your very best and as you move ahead you discover that work becomes fun. Want more fun? Then keep on learning. Learning becomes fun.

Eventually you will find yourself keeping up with the best. You might even pass the whole pack. Finding a passion is often a lifetime quest. It will reward you every day of your life if you pay the price of excellence.

The Wall

This morning at about a lap and a half around the mall I got this tired feeling. I felt as if I just could not make four laps. It reminded me of what a ball carrier often encounters on the three yard line of a National Football League game. They call it the goal line stand that he runs into and often he is stopped cold. Every now and then you see a play where the runner hits the wall, then he backs up a few feet and charges forward through a hole in the line to a touchdown. They call this second effort.

When I was a young man in Sapporo, Japan we had a gung ho general who was upset about the poor conditioning of his troops. He initiated a new physical fitness routine and every morning we would go for a march. Then on Friday he would have us jog or double time the last five miles.

At about two miles we would swear that we could not possibly run another two steps. We had this burning in our chest and our legs felt numb. We expected to drop from exhaustion. It seemed as if we were panting so hard that we would never get our breath. Then something strange happened.

We got what we called our second wind. From that point on things suddenly changed. Our legs seemed to go on automatic. The pain in our body subsided. The burning in our chest cooled down and we were able to run the rest of that five miles with relative ease.

I thought about that as I walked on through that second lap this morning. Oh, I didn't have a strong pain in my chest and I didn't ache all over. I felt strained enough to wonder if I'd make all four laps. Funny thing though, after two laps I felt strong. In fact, I completed five full laps this morning and it felt great.

I think I'll talk about that in Hawaii. How do you build a passion for safety? Perhaps you must learn to go for that second wind in a number of areas. In developing your safety programs. In winning the support of first, top management; then the support of employees.

It is always roughest just before that second wind kicks in and that is when most people quit. They used to have an ambulance and a truck following us on that five mile run. Often the ambulance and the truck would be filled with those who could not make it on their own.

Of course, the general knew that all of us could not make it and he ordered every person in our regiment to get out and try.

Second effort is really the key to breaking through all kinds of walls and barriers. I'm glad I made it through that second lap today. Perhaps I will attack a few other obstacles in my life today.

Depth of Field

*I*ce this morning and the roads were slick. I just bet we really don't get great spring weather here in Michigan until I get to Hawaii. That is okay with me; just so I am able to come out to the mall.

Debbie, an RN, took my blood pressure and it was 120 over 80 after my walk. I guess that is good and it made me happy. It doesn't take much to encourage me physically.

Mentally I am having a rough time getting in gear this morning. As I did my laps, different friends would join me and walk a while and the conversation did not allow me to do my daily visualization about Hawaii and those audiences we have scheduled.

I thought things would get better when I sat down to write, but I had hardly taken my pen in hand when an old timer came over to my table with a cup of coffee and settled in. He said, "I don't suppose I will bother you much." And I said, "I'm trying to write something." And he said, "That is perfectly all right." Then he proceeded to talk non-stop for fifteen minutes.

I finally gave up and came to the office. As I am working on my talk for the safety engineers I keep thinking about the idea of focusing in on safety. I have always been intrigued with cameras and quite a while back I was quite good with a camera. As I got better, I learned about focus and something called depth of field.

When you focus in on an object that is close to you then, generally speaking, objects which are a bit further from you will go out of focus. If you focus on the object further from you, then that near object will become a blur.

As I became more professional I discovered something called depth of field. What it means is that it is possible to add depth to the area that is in focus at one time. You do this by making the aperture of your camera smaller and giving the picture more time. It is a bit like a sand timer. The timer that lets sand flow through a hole to the area below. Some folks use them to time a two minute egg.

If you were to make that hole bigger then the sand would flow faster. Well, when you make the hole that the light comes through smaller and allow it to remain open longer then you will still get the same amount of light on the film. However, your picture will have more depth of field. Both those close objects and those a bit further back will now be in focus at the same time.

Likewise, I say that you can focus both on quality and on safety at the same time. It might take a bit more time and you must become more professional in what you are doing, but it is possible.

What many organizations learn is that when they do focus in on safety and develop an attitude of safety and caring within their group then they also get fringe benefits like higher quality, better worker attitudes and much more.

I'm working on that concept for the engineers. It is not a clear vision just yet in my mind's eye. But the picture is getting clearer and the talk is becoming more in focus.

Applause, Applause

My body is rebelling against me today. First it was my right knee that was bothering me at about a lap and a half. I talked myself through that one and the pain seemed to go away.

Next, it was my ankles, both of them. They hurt but I got through the second lap. It was well into the third lap when I heard a noise every time my right foot hit the ground. I was limping and so I stopped and took a quick drink at the fountain. Then I sat down and tightened the straps on my shoes. It worked just fine and I finished the third lap and then some. I didn't go for four laps because I didn't want to press my luck today.

Last night I was pushing the button on my television and I hit on *Wheel of Fortune*. It is not one of my favorite shows although some twenty million Americans watch it every day. I just watched the beginning where they introduced the host, Pat Sajak. They called out his name and the crowd cheered and cheered and the host acknowledged the applause again and again.

Jay Leno gets the same greeting each evening on his show and so does Dave Letterman. They walk on-stage and bask in that adulation. Now I am not suggesting that these folks do not have a certain talent, but come on now... Are they really that much better in their jobs than the plumber who came into my house recently and unplugged my drain? Certainly not.

What about that woman named Robin who cuts my hair? Robin does a great job, but I'll bet that neither Robin nor that plumber ever got that kind of applause that the television hosts receive every night.

As a professional speaker I receive applause both before and after my talks. Sometimes the audiences are quite generous and they give me a standing ovation. That seems unfair because, the truth is, most of the people in that audience will never receive a standing ovation in their entire lifetime.

In my talks recently I have tried to remedy this discrepancy by selecting a particular member of the audience and I entice the audience to give him or her a roaring, foot stomping standing ovation; just to celebrate the importance of the job the person and those like him or her do every day.

Often I write a special verse to celebrate that job and the people who do it. I have recently written such a verse titled Navy People for the audience I will be speaking for at Pearl Harbor. Here it is:

Navy People

America remains a land that's free
Because of Navy People
It's a safer world for you and me
Because of Navy People
And on the sea and in the air,
America remains supreme
Because of Navy People.
And we are free to live our dream
Because of Navy People
Yes, America stands proud and tall
Because you answered your Nation's call
And I salute you, one and all
Because you're Navy People!

Art Fettig (c) 1994

Heart

I believe it was the great Olympic gold medalist, pole vaulter Dave Wilkerson who said it, "Throw your heart over the crossbar and your body will follow." This morning I threw my heart over the crossbar five times. Well, it wasn't exactly a crossbar. I was doing sit ups this morning and I finally managed to do fifty without stopping.

That's right, a big five o. The last five took a lot of heart, believe me, but it was worth it. That is the first time I have managed to do fifty sit ups in many years and I feel that I am truly making some progress in preparing for our Hawaiian experience.

As I walked my three miles today I recalled an old story about a baby eagle whose parents were killed at the time of his birth. A farmer found the baby eagle and took him home and put him with his chickens. The chickens accepted the baby eagle and for some time the eagle walked around with the chickens feeling he was one of them.

Deep inside he was yearning to fly and to soar, but it was evident to him that chickens simply do not soar. One day a couple of eagles flying overhead spotted the eagle and after a bit they flew down and rescued the eagle. They spent some time with the young eagle and taught him to fly. Soon he was soaring through the sky with the other eagles.

I guess the moral of the story is that you can't fly and soar like an eagle if you hang around with a bunch of chickens, no matter what is inside you.

Most of the people I have met who are soaring, hang out with others who are flying high. That is why I am so enthusiastic about making this trip with Terry Pochert. Terry is a great videographer. He has many years experience at one of the best, most modern television studios in America.

In addition to that, he is an expert editor. He can stand with the best of them in an editing room and he has supervised many crews of camera people and editors. That is impressive, certainly, but that is not what makes Terry really special. What is unique about Terry is his genuine enthusiasm.

He goes into a project expecting something special to happen. Far too many video people go into a project expecting a disaster to happen and they are seldom disappointed. When things go wrong with Terry he just shrugs them off and overcomes them.

Terry throws his heart over the crossbar every time we shoot together. Terry is expecting some fantastic results in our video taping in Hawaii and so am I. After all, I'm soaring with an eagle.

Fire Power

In working on my safety talks for the U.S. Navy at Pearl Harbor I came upon some startling information. One Ohio class U.S. nuclear submarine carries more fire power that has been unleashed in all of the battles fought in the history of the world.

Let me run that by you again. One ship like the U.S.S. Georgia, when it goes to sea, carries the destructive forces greater than all of that unleashed in all of the battles in the world up to this point.

In World War II, three million tons of TNT (three megatons) were detonated. One nuclear sub carries fire power eight times that on a single cruise. If that shakes you up then consider this. The world stockpile of nuclear weapons is now equivalent to 8,000 World War II's.

Now I realize that that nuclear sub isn't going to have an incident and unleash all of that firepower accidentally. Nuclear power just doesn't work that way; but with the awesome potential for destruction it still provides me with the incentive to do all in my meager power to help prevent an accident on that or any other ship in the U.S. Navy.

Isn't it strange how the world and its people have come so far in their ability to destroy; yet, such a short distance to eliminate hunger, suffering and disease.

It is just a week from today that we fly from Detroit Metro to Hawaii. All of my programs are still a bit rough. Of course, if pushed I could go out and do any of those sessions right now but I'm far from satisfied. I know I can do them all better if I pay the price this coming week with greater effort.

Today I will search my files for a bit more pizzazz. I need more good humor. A line here, a line there, a bit more dressing to make it all more professional.

I'm walking outside this morning and I stopped at a mile and a half to write this material. Now I'll do the second mile and a half back home.

Just think, if we could change fire power to love power, what a wonderful world this would be.

Enthusiastic Arithmetic

A quick thirty minute walk in the woods and fifty-two, count them, fifty-two sit ups. Things are shaping up in the speech department. I'm settling in on each of the themes and adding the bits and pieces that will make the meetings sizzle.

One of the things I plan to do for the Navy is a segment I call *Enthusiastic Arithmetic*. I first learned it from a marvelous speaker named Alan Cimberg, who lives in Malverne, New York. Alan is a master when it comes to winning audience participation and building genuine enthusiasm within an organization. Rather than tell you what it is let me run you through it.

Simple Addition

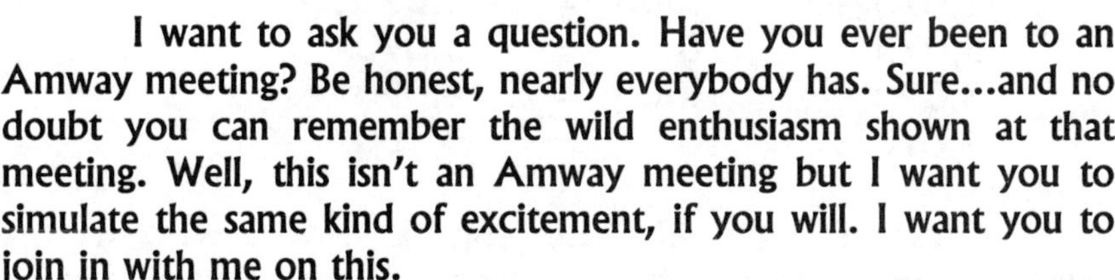

I want to ask you a question. Have you ever been to an Amway meeting? Be honest, nearly everybody has. Sure...and no doubt you can remember the wild enthusiasm shown at that meeting. Well, this isn't an Amway meeting but I want you to simulate the same kind of excitement, if you will. I want you to join in with me on this.

Before we go on with this, let me do a little research. Have you ever taken arithmetic? Certainly you have. Great! Right now, I want you to combine your enthusiasm and your mathematical expertise for a little experiment in simple addition. Let's go. I will give you the problem and you just say the number out loud with as much gusto as you can produce. Ready? Great! Just call out the answer...

Take one thousand and add forty. What is your answer?
>ONE THOUSAND AND FORTY!

Right. Now add a thousand. What did you get?
>TWO THOUSAND AND FORTY.

Fantastic. Now add thirty. What did you get?
>TWO THOUSAND SEVENTY.

Unbelievable...Let's add a thousand.
>THREE THOUSAND SEVENTY!

Great. Now add twenty. The answer?
>THREE THOUSAND NINETY!

Wonderful. Now add a thousand. The answer?
>FOUR THOUSAND NINETY!

Now add ten. What do you get?
>FIVE THOUSAND!

How much?
>FIVE THOUSAND?

One more time.
>FIVE THOUSAND?

Wrong! The answer is forty-one hundred. We had four thousand ninety and we added ten. That is forty-one hundred. Let's look at it:

1,000 +	40	=	1,040
1,040 +	1,000	=	2,040
2,040 +	30	=	2,070
2,070 +	1,000	=	3,070
3,070 +	20	=	3,090
3,090 +	1,000	=	4,090
4,090 +	10	=	4,100

Forty-one hundred is the correct answer. Now let me show you how modern education works. We have been running our system on something called "majority rule." The majority of people give the answer as five thousand. Now here's what we do. We change the questions so the answer will be right. After all, if everybody fails, then the teacher is stupid. I asked you the wrong questions. What I should have asked was this: "What is one thousand plus four hundred, not forty?" Plus a thousand and three hundred? Plus a thousand and two hundred? Plus a thousand and one hundred? Then the answer would be five thousand. Everyone passes and everyone would be happy. Then we go marching out of the classroom into this bright, big beautiful world. Everything is fine. Everybody is okay. That's what we've been doing in too many classrooms in America recently. That's why Johnny can't read and Mary can't spell, and why we're in big trouble in our educational system.

The same applies to safety. Some people think we bend the rules and we discover when we do we come up with the wrong results. When we ignore the safety rules people get hurt. So let's play it straight. Let's add up a string of accident-free days that we can all be proud of.

Growth

Oh it was rough today. Cramps in both of my feet and legs. I knew it was all in my mind, but I just could not talk my mind out of it today. I gave in after just three good laps.

I did my fifty-two sit ups first and it too was a struggle, but I made it. I just might take another walk later in the day if I manage to limber up.

This weekend I gave short talks at St. Philip Church, plugging a Christopher Leadership Course. It is an eight week success program starting tomorrow evening. My goal was to sign up twenty-five students and I managed to come up with twenty-five and two stand-by in case a couple dropped out.

I am very high on this course because I took the course in 1957 and it changed my life. It also got me up on my feet in front of an audience and I have never sat down since then. It was easy for me to highly endorse this course because the instructor was Jim Atkinson, one of the group's best and most experienced people.

I had four minutes to make my presentation at church and I concluded my remarks by telling the audience about a recent experience.

Just a few weeks ago, I was flipping my remote button on my television looking for something of interest. I came upon Art Linkletter's special on PBS. I watched a few moments and at the close of his show Art said that he'd like to close with a verse by his good friend, Art Fettig, a noted lecturer and author. I was thrilled.

Art Linkletter then recited my verse,*Growth*.

Growth

*I don't ever want to be
what I want to be.*

*There is always something
out there yet for me.*

*I get a kick from living
in the here and now.*

*Yet, I never want to feel
I've learned the best way how.*

*There is always one hill higher
with a better view.*

*Something waiting to be learned
that I never knew.*

*'Til my life is over
never fully fill my cup.*

Let me keep on growing.
                              Up!
                        Up!
                  Up!

Art Fettig (c) 1994

At the end of the poem I simply said, "If that verse makes sense to you and if you'd like more growth in your life, then I recommend you sign up for this wonderful course. They did. In Hawaii I will be using that verse with several of our audiences. It pretty well sums up my personal philosophy.

Remembering

*T*erry called yesterday and said, "I'm packed." I wish I could say that. I'm still moving my clothes around on my bed trying to figure out just what I should take.

I'm shuffling back and forth between two suitcases, in fact. One is big and heavy leather, built like a tank. The other is smaller and lighter and I have a feeling that the light one will win out.

I'm walking at noon today, sort of saving my energy. I was really pooped yesterday and my productivity was way down. I figured I'd get in a really good morning and then get my walking in.

We had a Fax from *Sacred Heart Academy* yesterday afternoon. They have our beautiful children all lined up and ready for our visit. They've asked me to do two assemblies, one for kindergarten through third grade. The second session is for the fourth through sixth grades.

One of the topics, memory, they have requested for the younger children, is from my book titled, *Remembering*. The book is based on the song, *This Old Man*. In this story, Billy, a young boy, believes that he has a broken memory. An old man explains to Billy that he has a wonderful memory, but that he simply has not learned to use it properly.

The old man gets Billy to sing the song, "This old man he played one. He played knick knack on my drum."

"That's it!" the old man exclaimed, "and drum is your first hook. All you have to do is hang your memories on those hooks through a ridiculous association."

Billy soon learned that he has ten memory hooks he knows from that song. One-drum, two-shoe, three-tree, four-door, five-hive, and so on. Next the old man asked Billy to tell him some of the things he wants to remember. Butter was the first.

"What is your memory hook for one?" the old man asked Billy.

"One is drum." Billy answered.

"That is right, Billy. What might we do with that butter that would be really silly?" said the old man.

"Let's smear it all over the drum." Billy suggested.

"You've got the idea," the old man said, "and let's put some butter on those drum sticks too, so they will slip out of your hands."

Two was shoe and Billy wanted to remember milk. "We'll pour the milk in my shoe," Billy said and they both laughed at the idea.

"Now this is all pretend," the old man said, "but let's pretend you put your shoe on with the milk in it."

"Ooh," said Billy, "that is cold."

In no time at all Billy had hung ten memories on the ten hooks he now had planted firmly in his mind.

I have used this story with children of all ages and the most fun of all is using the story with the elderly. Many older people feel badly because they believe they have lost their memories. It is really fun to tell the story to older people and watch their faces light up when, at the end of the story, they can all remember the ten hooks and the ten memories they hung on the hooks.

I know that Terry and I will have a wonderful time with these children. I'm having a ball just getting ready.

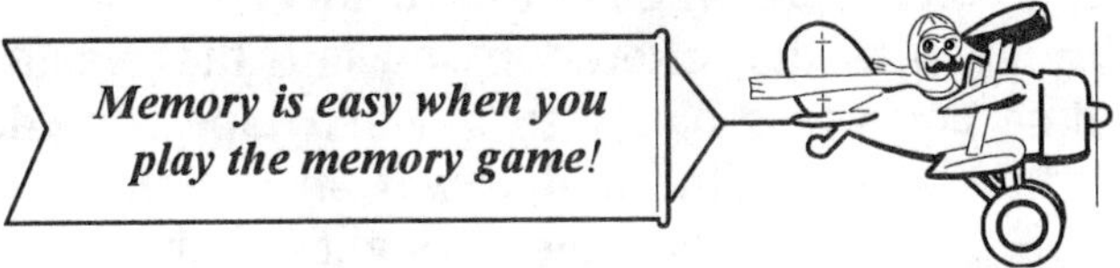

Good, Good, Good

I walked to church and back again this morning. At St. Philips they said a Mass for my late wife Ruthie. It was threatening rain and just a bit nippy, but it felt good to be walking outside.

I did my exercises earlier and managed another fifty-two sit ups. I wanted to work on my talk for speakers. There was one segment I call *Good, Good, Good* that I use with a wide variety of audiences, but it is most significant when I speak for speakers.

Many years ago, when I first made the commitment to become a professional speaker, I received a brochure announcing a day and a half seminar to be conducted by Cavett Robert, the founder of the National Speaker's Association. The price was $550 and I knew I would also have the expense of two nights in a fancy Chicago hotel plus meals and gas for my car.

At that time we had four kids at home and that was a great deal of money to us. I decided that it was an investment in my future and so I signed up for the seminar.

There were twenty-five attendees, all of us aspiring professional speakers in different stages of our careers. Cavett explained that he would lecture for half a day and then we would spend the afternoon video taping each of us as we delivered our best ten minutes of material. Then the following morning he would give us a critique on our performance.

We taped all that afternoon and into the evening. It was the first time any of us had seen a video tape recorder. They were very new at that time and it was an exciting experience. More exciting, though, was the thought of the great Cavett

Robert doing a personal critique on our work. Many of the other speakers, like me, could not sleep that night it was so thrilling.

The next morning, following breakfast, we all gathered in the meeting room with great expectations and Cavett walked to the front of the room and pressed the button on the video machine. The picture came on the screen and there was no sound. Cavett adjusted the sound control on the television and tried again. Once more there was no sound. He called in the television technician and after puttering around with the connections and the other equipment for ten minutes he finally announced, "Mr. Robert, I'm sorry but somehow you didn't get any sound when you recorded all that stuff yesterday."

We all looked at Cavett and then we looked at each other. It was a disaster. Cavett calmly tugged at his shirt cuffs and said quietly, "Good, good, good!" Then he raised his head and smiled and repeated it only much louder this time, "GOOD, GOOD, GOOD!"

Next he looked around the room for an instant and asked, "How many of you have audio tapes of your talks?" Of course, we all had audio tapes of our talks. Most of us taped every talk we did and then spent painful hours listening to the results.

"Well then, I don't think this is a problem." Cavett explained. "Over the years, I have learned that it isn't so much what you say to an audience that matters. It is more how you feel deep down inside your gut that matters. No matter how slick you get at saying anything it will not come through to that audience unless you really feel it inside."

"Good, Good, Good." He repeated and when he did I realized that I had heard him say that on other occasions, especially when something went wrong. That was Cavett's way of reminding himself that there was something good in anything that happened if you would only take a moment to look for it.

"What we will do," Cavett told us, "is play those tapes back without the sound and see what really comes through." My partner, Merlyn Cundiff, is an expert on body language and she will help me with the critiques." What happened then was a life changing experience. We'd all heard each other's talks and we pretty well remembered what was said but looking at those videos without the sound gave us a new perspective.

When the meeting had ended, everyone of us had a whole new understanding about what professional speaking is all about. It is about caring and about commitment and about honesty, too. "It is as if you are standing naked in front of an audience," Cavett explained. "Unless you are genuine they will see it and your message will not touch their hearts."

Each of us went home with a new determination to purge our talks of anything that was not true and absolutely sincere. At that seminar we all learned how to talk from our hearts and nearly everyone who attended that session became a successful professional speaker in the years that followed.

Good, Good, Good. That just might be the most important message I can share with those speakers. So many would be speakers try to deceive an audience and it simply does not work. Honesty and integrity and caring are critical if you hope to really touch people's lives. If I can get that idea across to that audience of speakers then the whole trip will be worthwhile.

Volunteers

Today's exercise is a full day seminar with volunteers. I'll be on my feet four hours this morning and the way I move around while speaking I bet I get in three or four miles. My gestures alone will give me a real workout.

What might I tell volunteers? That they are wonderful? Yes. That this whole nation would collapse without them? Of course. But maybe it will be easier if I just shared with you a verse that I wrote for volunteers.

The Volunteer

Give a cheer, give a cheer, for the Volunteer
For while others say they'll see to it,
Give a cheer, give a cheer for the Volunteer
For they simply go out and do it.

Give a cheer, give a cheer, for the Volunteer
They are brave and they're ready for scrappin'.
Give a cheer, give a cheer, for that Volunteer,
They're the people who make good things happen.

Give a cheer, give a cheer, for the Volunteer
I think God sends them down from above.
Give a cheer, give a cheer, for the Volunteer
Yes, they fill this whole world full of love.

Art Fettig

I'm here at a wonderful log bed and breakfast on a beautiful lake and people will be here to meet with me in just a few moments. Breakfast at 7:30 A.M., registration at 8:30 A.M. and we start at 9:00 A.M. 120 dedicated people who share one interest. The giving of a part of themselves and their lives just to make this a better community and a better world.

Becky Beets, a wonderful woman who works with the Newaygo County Foster Grandparent Program first contacted me about this program. I met Becky many years ago when I spoke for a toy company and we've been friends ever since.

Co-host was Lana Ford, County Extension Director in Newaygo County for *Michigan State University*. Both women proved to be great to work with because of their total dedication to public service.

This is a good warm up day for me getting ready for Hawaii. I'll get the cobwebs out of my entire system and start my communications channels cooking.

The weather is warming up today and so am I. Ladies and gentlemen, start your engines. The main event is just about to begin. *It's Showtime.*

Last Minute Stuff

Yesterday was a perfect warm-up for our trip. The audience was fantastic and my speaking skills are now honed to a fine edge.

I broke out my new Panama hat this morning and really shook up those people at *Roger The Chef's* restaurant. I'm walking outside at noon today and the weather is finally warm and wonderful, just in time for me to leave Michigan for Hawaii. But in Michigan, who knows, it just might be snowing again tomorrow.

Packing today. Last minute shopping, a drive to Terry's home this evening and tomorrow morning at 7:00 A.M. *Aloha!*

I have a feeling deep inside that this will prove to be the most productive, rewarding, enjoyable and exciting trip of my lifetime.

Enroute

Grapefruits at 4:30 A.M., at Terry's. We had some final packing to do with a real load of video gear including cordless mikes, rechargeable batteries and such.

We are now a walking video studio and safely aboard American flight 797 enroute to Dallas, Texas. We change planes there for a direct flight non-stop to Honolulu.

So far, everything has gone like clockwork. My own apprehension was whether we could take possession of the boxes of books and things we'd shipped ahead by U.S. mail. A message from Don King on my answering machine last night informed me that everything had arrived safely. He also said that he would deliver them to the location of my choice this weekend.

So perfect. Yes, so far everything seems special on this trip. Both Terry and I have aisle seats and we have three seats each to stretch out on.

My exercise regime seems a bit neglected today, so far. Hopefully we will get in a great walk on a beach later today. Last night we stopped at *J.C. Penney's* and I picked up a pair of khaki slacks. Darned if I didn't have to buy two sizes smaller in the waist line.

What a joy to fit into smaller clothes. Especially when I realize that it has happened in less than three weeks, since I started to write this book. Those daily sit-ups hurt but they helped me a lot.

We are over the Pacific Ocean now at this moment. It is 7:15 A.M. in Honolulu. That means we still have over five more hours of flying on this eight hour flight. We have eaten and the movie will be starting soon.

Terry and I have been discussing video production and our minds are swirling around with great new ideas. When we start brainstorming together there is a wonderful synergism that doubles and triples the value of the ideas we create on an individual basis. Later as we put some of these ideas together to work in our video production, I will share some of these new ideas that we come up with.

On our trip from Detroit to Dallas this morning our imaginations were soaring as we discussed some new concepts in the field of safety. I noticed that a passenger sitting behind us seemed to become more and more interested in our conversation. Finally, when we started talking about the value of safety teams that gentleman could no longer contain himself.

He took out his business card, leaned forward and introduced himself. He was Christopher Herman, safety team leader from *British Petroleum Oil's* Toledo, Ohio refinery. He joined our discussion and we had a marvelous time. Terry and I plan to follow up with him because he is a real safety professional that we both want to know better.

We just spotted land and we are like a couple of kids with anticipation. Terry whipped out his computer enroute and did a lot of constructive work. I visited with a beautiful lady from Hawaii. Her name is Pono and she is a former Miss Hawaii and a popular singer in Hawaii. It amazes me how friendly people can be if you only give them half a chance.

Fasten your seatbelts and put your seats in an upright position for our final approach. We are just about fifteen minutes early. Beautiful Oahu is just beneath us. Ladies and Gentlemen,

ALOHA!

Touring the North Shore

*A*bsolutely overwhelming. That is what the beauty of Hawaii is. We are walking the beaches today, *Sunset Beach* and *Kaihalulu*. Last night we went to the *Polynesian Culture Center* and we pigged out at a Luau. We saw an unbelievable movie on Polynesia, and then a spectacular live show.

Hula, hula, hula. Let's say that last night there was a whole lot of shaking going on. We stopped off at *Waimea Falls Park* and watched the high divers. The park is a real adventure with trees and flowers of every description.

Frankly, I am running out of adjectives to describe Hawaii. Fabulous, enchanting, breathtaking. Terry has been shooting a bit of scenery and he tells me that he can point his camera in any direction and come up with postcard scenery.

As we waited for the divers to perform we talked shop and ran through all of the programs we have scheduled. I went through some of my kids routines with Terry and then we discussed camera positions and such. A few such moments of preplanning can prevent a lot of regrets later. Nearly everything we are doing must be done right the first time. We will both have to be at our top form all week to make this schedule a real success.

We are checking into the *Outrigger Reef Hotel* here on *Waikiki Beach*. It is a nice hotel with a great beach and an interesting restaurant called the *Shore Bird Beach Broiler*. We broiled our own fish on their huge pits and then hogged down on salad, going really heavy on the fresh pineapple.

We visited the *Dole Pineapple Plantation* earlier and wolfed down at least a gallon of fresh pineapple juice. We need all the nourishment we can muster and now all of the rest.

It is 9:00 P.M. and Terry is already asleep. So I will turn this off right now. Tomorrow, yes it is true, tomorrow at 9:00 A.M. at the *Sacred Heart Academy*, it is *Showtime.*

Joy

I think that the most exciting thing for me all day was watching Terry with those wonderful children at *Sacred Heart Academy*, a famous old Hawaiian girls school established in 1909. Our hostess was Nancy Goglia, and the cooperation we received was unbelievable.

We met with both the school principal, Mrs. Betty White and the vice principal, Mrs. Remee Bolante and received a really warm welcome from them. We had a rainbow of races in ages running from five to twelve; mostly girls, but a nice sprinkling of boys from *St. Patrick's School* across the street. It was a real joy to watch Terry Pochert take charge of about forty children and turn a video project into a really fun event. Needless to say, the taping of the *Karaoke Just Say Yes Rap* video was a wonderful, memorable experience for both of us.

We were guided to the school auditorium where we had two assemblies scheduled. The first was with the children from grades kindergarten through third grade. Children that age are marvelous. They still have unbounded imagination and when you tell them stories they listen to every word. They are such fun to work with, they listened to our songs and sang along on cue.

Thirty minutes is plenty of time for such an audience, yet I held them for an hour with ease. The second audience was a bit more of a challenge. This was fourth through sixth grades. I decided to do my *Enthusiastic Arithmetic* routine with them. When they all shouted, "Five thousand," which was the incorrect answer, I managed to turn it into a lesson on peer pressure.

We talked about smoking cigarettes, softly about chastity and I felt I had a real impact on them. I shared my verse titled *Somebody* which goes:

Somebody

I'm not the right height,
And my face is a mess
I'm not good at sports,
And I'll never play chess.
My grades aren't the highest,
And it's easy to see,
But I'm happy to tell you
I'm glad to be me.

I'm somebody special,
Just one of a kind,
I'm unique, with a greatness,
I'm seeking to find.
I'm happy, I'm healthy,
I'm somebody, true,
And I'm sure glad to say,
That you're somebody too!

Art Fettig (c) 1987

I had written that poem especially for fifth and sixth graders. When children reach the impossible age of adolescence they feel that everything about them is wrong. Their height, their weight, their bodies, their faces; I felt they needed to be reminded they are really beautiful and marvelous and lovable.

I told them just that. I told them I was at their school that day because I truly believed they were the most beautiful school children in the world. I meant that statement from my heart. The Hawaiian children represent most every race in the world: Blacks, Whites, Japanese, Hawaiian, Chinese, Vietnamese and just about every other race you can think of.

Those children were so loving and kind to one another. It made me wish we could bottle up all that love and share it with the children in every school in this world.

We visited the U.S. Navy at Pearl Harbor in the afternoon. We firmed up our plans for the program and video taping the following morning. Before sunset we met with vivacious Nan Hanson, a Career Development Specialist, who hosted our program for the members of the Hawaiian Chapter of the National Speaker's Association on the top floor of the *Ala Moana Business Building*.

They call this the magic island and the view of the sunset outside was spectacular. I think Terry was far more impressed with the magnificent sunset outside than he was with my presentation. I must say they both went right on schedule and the audience was most gracious.

I am glad we scheduled the program because it gave us the opportunity to meet some wonderful people like Ruth E. Heidrich, a Ph.D. who rode her bicycle to the meeting. She is a talk show host on nutrition and was on the All-American Triathlon team. We met Myrna Zezza, a lovely woman, who talks about how to build a loving relationship, and Susan Luke, the dynamic President-elect of the group.

It was really inspiring to have so many celebrities in that group and Terry captured it all with his camera. By the time we ate and reached the hotel we were both exhausted. Later Terry and I sat on our beds grinning at one another.

We were both full of appreciation for a perfect day, that it was, somehow, beyond words. We sort of glowed from the loving warmth of those wonderful kids and the speakers we had met.

The power of the breathtaking view of the sunset had deeply moved us both. What a sensational *Showtime* it had been for us and now we needed sleep.

Showtime was 8:00 A.M. at Pearl Harbor for the United States Navy.

Terry

Art

Remember Pearl Harbor

Yes, we will remember Pearl Harbor for a long time. Terry and I arrived early and met with Suzanne Fujii who was our hostess. We had Mark Hansen, Suzanne's boss, assigned to helping us plus a couple of other enlisted men.

The video taping went exceptionally well. Terry and I both feel that the magic was really there for the entire program. The audience was hot-hot-hot and so was I.

There was a tragic incident in Northern Iran on Thursday. The *USA Today's Weekend Edition* carried the headline, "Screwups Kill 26." Two Air Force F15's based in nearby Turkey identified two helicopters as Iraqis' violating the "no fly zone" over Kurdish areas and fired air to air missiles.

"It sounds to me like a series of major screwups," says Peter Wilson of the *Rand Company*. Early reports were citing pilot error. As I talked for the Navy personnel I asked them how many had read of the incident. They all had. I asked them how many would do everything in their power to prevent such a disaster. Of course, they all would.

USA Today had several other examples of incidents where Americans had been killed by so called "friendly fire." They cited the July 2, 1988 tragedy when the U.S.S. Vincennes shot down Iran Air Flight 655 over the Persian Gulf. The plane, mistaken for an attacking fighter, was hit by an air to air missile killing 290.

A *Detroit Free Press* story about the U.S.S. Vincennes incident said the following:

"A psychologist who recently reexamined the incident for the Navy found that a 'staggering number of things went wrong.' For example it was learned that a computer design flaw misled the captain about the airliner's course. Some Vincennes crew members realized that the captain was getting incorrect information but were reluctant to speak up. As a result, the captain believed the approaching aircraft was descending toward the Vincennes and ordered his crew to fire."

My whole presentation was about making a personal commitment to safety and to positive interaction. It was about giving others permission to positively interact with others whenever they believed you were behaving in an unsafe manner.

As I read that *Free Press* article it suddenly struck me that just possibly, if my concept had been adopted by the U.S. Navy prior to that Vincennes incident, maybe one of those Navy personnel might have positively interacted with the captain in time. He may have cried out, "Captain, you are getting incorrect information."

I'm trying to break down the barriers which prevent us from protecting one another from disaster. I watched the line up of Navy people as they waited patiently to sign our *Declaration of Interdependence for Safety*, to make their own personal commitment to safety and positive interaction. As I watched, I silently prayed that sometime, somewhere, someone would have the courage to forget about race or rank or age or seniority and step forward and say, "This is not right. Someone is going to get killed and it is not necessary."

I really felt comfortable with that audience and they were very supportive and cooperative. I believe we have six videos. I also feel they have the stuff to win acceptance throughout the U.S. Navy. That was our goal and right now I see no reason why we cannot reach it if we find the right marketing approach.

We got back to *Waikiki Beach* in plenty of time to leisurely set up our books and for me to put the final touches on my talk for the Safety Engineers. The title of my talk for the Safety Engineers is *"Keeping the Passion for Safety Alive."* I had prepared to use a different close, but for some reason I changed my mind. I had recently seen that very special movie titled *Schindler's List.*

In the movie, Schindler, a Nazi, had opened a munitions plant to make his fortune. At first he gave jobs to the Jews for his own selfish reasons. As time passed he realized that he was actually saving the lives of his employees. In all, he saved the lives of 1,200 Polish Jews. Somehow he could not bear to turn out weapons of war, so he arranged to produce only defective weapons.

Soon the Army refused to pay him, so he began to use up the fortune he had accumulated, just to keep the plant going and to employ more Jews. At the end of the movie the war has ended and Schindler explains to his workers that he must flee himself, since he is a Nazi.

As a sign of their appreciation and love, the Jewish workers have the gold extracted from their teeth in order to make a gold ring as a parting gift. Schindler is deeply moved by the gift. As he leaves the plant, he suddenly sees his automobile sitting there.

"The auto," he says. "Why did I keep the auto? I might have sold it and saved several more lives." Suddenly Schindler realized that he could have done more.

My final challenge to the audience of Safety Engineers was this, "Ladies and Gentlemen, I hope that none of you will ever ask yourselves why you haven't done more to save a life or prevent an accident. I challenge you to develop a continuing passion for safety in your life."

The audience was attentive and loving and we sold a pile of books after my talk. Terry tells me that the video taping went very well. We both feel very confident about the project to date.

Terry and I attended a cocktail party on the hotel lawn later. We caught a ride with Jane Conroy, the wife of Pat Conroy, our host for the safety meeting and we headed for a great Chinese restaurant. Jane is a special woman. Did you ever meet someone who is so kind and loving and understanding that you'd swear you had known her all your lifetime? Someone who is instantly a very special person? Well, that is Jane Conroy.

The food was fabulous. We dined with Herman Woessner, President of *SafeRisk Corporation* and his wife,

Aline and with Jim and Jan Hinson. The conversation was superb. Jim has an organization called *J. Hinson Network, Inc.*, in Foster City, California. Jim is a consultant, a fine speaker, and a safety engineer and risk manager. The dinner was the perfect topping on one of the two most rewarding days of my life.

Before dinner Terry and I had set up our exhibit booth at the hotel. We were ready for the ribbon cutting and the opening of the exhibit hall for the attendees at the Governor's Pacific Rim Safety and Health Conference.

I went to sleep the instant before my head hit the pillow. I was totally exhausted, but I really felt happy this day, happier than I have felt for perhaps a couple of years.

Yes, it was two years ago since my wife, Ruthie, was here in Hawaii with me. She'd been suffering with recurrent cancer for many years and this time she had somehow overcome liver cancer and seemed to be well again. It was a fantastic trip we had to Hawaii. Then after we returned home and shared six more months of happiness, Ruthie came down with cancer once again.

It was a tough battle and Ruthie fought it bravely but finally, in June of the following year she passed away. We had been married nearly thirty-nine years.

I'd been in a sort of limbo since then and yet, bit by bit I was getting back on track. Happiness had been sort of a stranger to me though. So when I talk about really feeling happy it represents a breakthrough for me.

This beautiful land with its loving charm has wrapped its magic healing fingers around my life and somehow made it better.

Meeting The People

*T*oday started out with a great event. We opened our exhibit booth with a bang! Within fifteen minutes of opening our booth we sold out of the paperback copies of our safety books.

Of course, we had both audio and video tapes on safety, and books and tapes on public speaking. We also had whole kits for kids and parents; so we had a great time with the visitors to our booth. It was fantastic when people would come up and say they'd heard me two years ago or four years ago or the day before and that I had touched their lives.

Terry listened to a lot of these wonderful testimonials and then he got the brilliant idea of setting up his camera and getting some of these stories on tape. We had a great time of it doing these interviews with visitors.

Exhibiting is exhausting work and yet it is really good to spend time with both meeting attendees and the other exhibitors too. You get a feel for the safety profession and industry as well as great feedback on what people are most concerned with today.

In Hawaii there are a number of concerns. High living costs are a major problem. There is a continuing recession in both the tourist and the construction industry. Most of all, Terry and I discovered the people are polite, caring, loving and wonderful to work with.

We had scheduled a talk for the Rotary today but something happened and it was canceled. Of course, we were disappointed but that is all part of the speaking business.

A while back I thought it was right to just fly into a city, give a talk and then get back to an airport as quickly as possible. I guess I'm mellowing. Now I really enjoy taking my time and visiting with as many people at a meeting or convention as possible. I find that every person has something valuable to contribute if you only take the time to listen.

Terry went for a swim before dinner. Then we went out to a great buffet where we ate wonderful food. We turned in early, exhausted and ready for some needed sleep.

Exhibiting

*I*t is absolutely exhausting manning a booth at a conference. After a couple of days of this your back hurts, your legs hurt, and if you are not careful your feelings might be hurt too. I think that manning a booth should be a required activity for anyone studying human behavior.

Actually the attendees in Hawaii might serve as models for a nice people category. They are polite, caring and for the most part real human beings. In other words, they are so unlike the people you meet while attending most exhibits.

At a conference where I manned a booth in Chicago, many of the attendees act like actual zombies who are having a bad day. Often they walk down the center of the aisles between booths staring straight ahead, ignoring the booths as they pass. They act as if they are looking for a beach somewhere ahead. If you speak to them as they pass they fake deafness.

Today here at the *Sheraton Waikiki*, many of the attendees stopped at our booth at least to say hello. Some shared marvelous examples of how my talks and seminars had touched their lives. Some thanked me for the continuing inspiration which my quarterly newsletter provides.

What I really thrive on at safety conferences is the personal contact with other presenters. Often they stop at our booth and we trade war stories.

Richard Hislop who is Associate Director of the Environmental Safety and Health Division at *Argonne National Lab* in Illinois stopped by our booth and I learned a lot about construction safety.

An old friend, Herb Everett, known worldwide as "Safety Herb" stopped by. We talked about his really great safety program for *Westmark Hotels* throughout Alaska. Herb has been using our books and video tapes for years and he is a real inspiration.

We got to shake hands with Leonard Ring, the famous ergonomist from Auckland, New Zealand. He is famous for his groundbreaking work in preventing repetitive motion injuries.

Then Richard Kephart, Ph.D. from Dixon, California stopped by and we swapped experiences on building great safety teams. His wife, Helaine, also a wonderful speaker was with him.

All of these folks were presenters at the Safety Conference. It is an opportunity for all of us to share and learn.

Judy Ward, Vice President of *Ergo Tech International* stopped by our booth the first day and I learned she is a former teacher working with schools bringing the ergonomic technology of the future into classrooms. She's committed to preventing injuries to children caused by improper equipment.

I felt drawn to Judy and I gave her a copy of a tape of one of my talks titled *Teacher-Teacher*. The next morning she stopped by my booth to say that her mother was very ill and that she had played the tape for her and it had been a real blessing. I then autographed my book titled *Serenity! Serenity!* for her mother. The next morning she was there again at the booth with her heartfelt thanks. The book had really given her mother the courage to go on with her battle against disease. These are the things that make exhibiting special.

Perhaps the major reason that exhibiting in Hawaii is so easy and rewarding is a man named George Mauliola from GASPRO. George is in charge of the exhibits and he made everything easier. His crew was there when we were setting up and George came by our booth every day to see that things were going well. He also provided the best security for our booths that I have ever seen. It is such a joy to work with true professionals.

Both Terry and I enjoyed our experience exhibiting. Later after a quick dinner we went to our room and Terry worked on his computer, registering the information we'd picked up and the requests for various information and such.

I worked on my speech for the Governor's Conference Breakfast the next day. I shuffled through several hundred notes and eliminated a ton of stuff I'd really like to include in my presentation. I cut and cut and cut again. I moved the cribs on various stories around again eliminating a wealth of materials.

It was nearly 10:30 P.M. and we must be up at five. Finally I made one more cut and I put the material that had survived the many cuts into a folder for the following morning.

Terry was in bed looking very much asleep. "There," I said to him, "I've finally got it down to about four hours." It was true and I had at most only forty minutes for my talk. Down to four hours. It struck me funny and I laughed out loud. After all these weeks of planning I finally had the talk down to four hours.

I'd cut tomorrow on stage by taking from that four hours of great stuff and do my level best to fill the real needs of that audience in the time I had been given. I prayed for guidance. I prayed for wisdom. I prayed that my love would shine through. Then I slept.

I would leave a lot of the final cut of that four hours of material up to my subconscious mind.

Showtime at Last

*T*he phone rang at 5:00 A.M. "Thank you for calling and let's both make it a great day." Terry said. Then he hung up the phone and said to me, "I can't believe that real people still make calls to wake you up in this hotel. They are at least five years behind in their automation."

"Yes," I agreed, "But they certainly are nice and they talk back to you in a friendly manner and answer questions instead of just going click." We were off to what will probably be the best day of the whole adventure. At 6:00 A.M. we set up our table in the room that was prepared for our breakfast.

We got into the conference headquarters office where we had stored everything the night before. Terry began setting up his camera. I set out our boxes of tapes and books. After that things seemed to go into high gear. Terry put on my cordless mike transmitter and we checked it out. Then I checked out the hall mikes and the stage lighting came on.

I met with Pat Conroy, the Conference Program Chairperson and we went over the introduction. Pat is probably the best program chairperson I have had the honor to work with. He covers every detail in a professional manner. Because of this, things are right every time. He gave me a lovely plaque as a memento. He reminded me that a pretty woman would put a lei around my neck and I should wait for it before I started speaking.

I put my notes on the lectern and went out to the back of the hall. I filled a plate with fresh fruit and a couple of tasty rolls. The waitress had set each table with copies of my *Growth* poem for the attendees. I ate quickly and visited with John P. Souza, the Vice-president of the Association. He is a wonderful, caring guy who really gets things done.

We agreed that I could talk until 8:07 A.M. Then Pat suggested that it would be really special if I could close at 8:00 A.M. and get the crowd into the other room for one more visit with the vendors. The people had eaten. Pat was making announcements. My motor was running. I checked my watched. I had a good forty minutes if I got right on.

Pat introduced a lady for an honor, named Yvonne Yamashita. She was presented with a plaque for her valuable contribution to the success of the convention by co-chairpersons, Don King of *King and Neel, Inc.* and Jennifer Shishido. Then another man spoke briefly. There were prize drawings, another little speech. I was down to thirty-five minutes, then thirty, and then I was on. I did a little humor. A serious line, a challenge. My talk was titled, *"Winning the Commitment for Safety."* I decided to tell them about Captain James Cook of the British Navy. I had discovered this story in the wonderful book titled *Alaska,* by author James Michener.

He told that in 1778 a man named James Cook was placed in charge of a British warship. Before Cook, a British warship could leave England with a crew of 400 sailors and expect 180 to be dead by the time the voyage was over. Sometimes the toll reached the appalling figure of 280.

I asked the audience to imagine that they were on Cook's crew and that he had called a meeting on safety and health. Cook was standing on the poop deck as he talked to the assembled crew below.

"Men," he began. "On a ship like this we could expect that on this voyage, 180 of you would die. If we have rough weather or such, then 280 would normally die." Then Cook would look down at the 400 men and section the group off saying, "180 would be about from here on over and 280 would be from here on over." Then with a broad gesture he would say, "About that many of you would be expected to die."

Looking very solemn he would say, "However, I have come up with some rules for your safety and health. If everyone of you follow the rules, then nobody must die. How many of you will listen to the rules?"

I then turned to the audience and asked, "How many of you believe you would be willing to listen under those circumstances?" The entire audience raised their hands.

Cook went on to list his rules:

First, keep your quarters clean.
Second, wear dry clothes whenever you can.
Third, follow our rule of one watch on, two off.
Get plenty of rest.
Finally, you will each day consume your portion of wort
and rot.

"Say what?" He explained that each of them was expected to take a slug of wort, a mixture of malt, sauerkraut and whatever vegetables they might toss into the pot. Rot was a mixture of lime and orange juice.

The crew agreed and later they became known as "Limeys", because of the drink they had each day to insure their health. By this simple process, scurvy was conquered and the British Navy went on to greater fame and glory.

Captain Cook became a legend in his own time. Unfortunately, on a visit to Hawaii, he and his crew outstayed their welcome and when his ship had problems they returned to Hawaii for repairs. The natives had had their fill and Cook was killed.

Now I asked the audience of Safety Conference attendees this question. "What if, in my forty-six years of experience in the safety field, while working with many of the top safety people and major corporations, I had come up with a special pill? If everyone would simply take this pill in the morning, then no one would ever be injured on the job again. How many of you could persuade every employee to take the pill just as Captain Cook persuaded his crew to follow his rules?"

Again, the audience responded. Then I had to admit that I had no such pill. I did have a program that obtains a personal, signed commitment to safety and to positive interaction from every member of an organization. "But before you can win a commitment to safety from anyone you must first make your own personal and total commitment to safety."

I don't know what else I did. I poured some water on the floor to make a point. My subconscious was in control, cutting, customizing, reaching out with words that came from deep in my heart.

I thanked so many of them for their constant support during the period when my Ruthie was dying and then afterwards. I was just getting into it when I checked my watch and it was 7:55 A.M. "My God, time to close," I thought silently. "Wouldn't it be great if I could get out of this exactly on time? Wouldn't it really be professional if I could also give the vendors a strong plug and get the audience into the next room immediately?"

I did my *Growth* poem. I passed up all the stuff that leads to standing ovations. I spun my magic yarns and as I hit that last line of thanks I looked down at my watch. The second hand was straight up exactly on the twelve, right on the money.

I'd brought it in right on time. It was done in twenty nine minutes flat. It was a ten. I knew it was a ten. Terry knew it was a ten, and he knew that he had a ten in shooting that video, too. Two tens out of two possible tens.

We both went quickly to the product table. I signed poems and books and listened to a hundred people tell me they'd laughed and cried. That somehow I had touched their lives. Most important, instead of wanting to tell me how great I was, they simply wanted to say, "Thank you" for something precious I had given them.

It was a little after 8:00 A.M. now and this precious day was just beginning. I'll tell you more about it tomorrow.

Capturing

*I*t is Saturday, the day we travel on to Maui. Before we go, I must capture those awesome memories of yesterday. After breakfast Terry and I moved our remaining videos and books back to the exhibiting area. At noon we packed up a couple of boxes and went directly to the post office to ship them home.

We ate a quick lunch and went back to the hotel for some rest. At 3:00 P.M. we were up, ready for a great adventure. Terry drove to the *Royal Hawaiian Hotel* where we picked up our new friends, Jim and Jan Hinson, who live in San Francisco.

For some reason Jan gave Terry the nickname, Oppy and she called me Andy. Somehow she felt we both belonged on the *Andy Griffith Show*. I guess we both do look the part. Anyhow, the nicknames set the tone for what was about to happen. Our mission was to climb to the top of *Diamond Head*. We found the starting point and began our climb with high hopes. Much of the trail is paved and I guess we were half way up when I started panting a bit.

We moved on and I must admit it was a great physical challenge. Near the top we walked through this long, dark tunnel with Terry leading the way with his camera light. At one point he shut off the light, then he turned it on with it shining on his face, which wore a hideous expression. He let out a ghastly yell and the effect was perfect.

We plodded on and once we got through that tunnel we faced a stairway of about ninety-seven steps. It was here that I really began to thank God for those warm up walks at the mall each morning. Up those steps I treaded and when I'd conquered those I faced yet another stairway of forty more.

Maybe it was the elevation but I was really exhilarated. After the final forty steps I knew I would conquer that mountain. Finally, we came to a bunker and we looked out on an absolutely fabulous scene. We climbed through the front of the bunker. As we came around the corner of some rocks, a wonderful cool breeze greeted us.

It wasn't difficult from there. A few more steps to the top, then I scooted myself on to the highest rock. I stood there holding my hands high above my head, truly the conquering hero. It felt magnificent. It was a moment of great personal triumph. For some reason I cannot explain I sensed that this was another turning point in my life.

My time of mourning had ended. It was now time to get on with the rest of my life. It was time to play and to have fun. It was a wonderful moment of joy. The steps I'd climbed were symbolic of the horror I'd been through with Ruthie's suffering and then the sorrow of our sixteen year old step-grand daughter, Marina's death.

Coming through that dark tunnel into the glorious sunshine, standing atop that stone looking down on beautiful Oahu, filled my heart with a happiness I had not felt for many years. As I stood at the top of *Diamond Head* I made a silent vow that I would return to celebrate my 75th birthday to climb it again. It sounds like a really major accomplishment to shoot for. Then on our way down we met a group of Japanese men and one told us he was celebrating his 80th birthday. He told us he had just finished playing eighteen holes of golf. I still plan to return. For me it will be a real physical accomplishment.

Now I was thirsty, really thirsty and there was a group of girls with a bottle of cool clear water. One by one they all had a satisfying drink. I went up to them and asked if I might have a small swallow to ease my parched throat. Lorna Stonewall, a lovely young lady from San Francisco generously handed me the bottle and said, "Take it, it is all yours."

I took a small swallow and offered it to my friends, but they all declined. So I took a good swallow and it was gone.

Again I thanked Lorna and her friends. That passage from the bible came to my mind, "I was thirsty and you gave me to drink."

Now after drinking in that breathtaking scene again, we congratulated one another. Then we began the easy journey down. On the steps Jan called out, "One, two." That got me started with the Jodie Cadences. "Sound off!" Jim and Jan and Terry bellowed back, "One, two." We were off.

"Ain't no use to goin' home
Jodie's got your gal and gone
Ain't no use to goin' back
Jodie's got your Cadillac.
Sound off."

Now they really bellowed back, "One, two." It went on like that all afternoon. That little kid in us was loose and so were we. We skipped together through a shopping center. We played follow the leader. Jan challenged us to a race to *Baskin Robbins* with "the last one is ugly." Jan was ugly and we all let her know this, loud and clear, in no uncertain terms. Actually, she is a youthful, beautiful woman and she brought out the little kid in us.

When I paid for our ice cream and came outside, they were all hiding behind a post. We dined on chili with pop. At *Radio Shack* in the mall, Terry found a video connector for his two inch television screen.

Later at our hotel we went through all of the video tapes. They are absolutely unbelievable. The color is perfect. The sound is out of this world. The children at *Sacred Heart Academy* are gorgeous. We did it all on Oahu: great video, great shows, and the people were fantastic. What glorious *Showtimes* we shared. Today we fly to Maui. It's Playtime!

Maui

Yesterday we moved from Oahu to Maui on Aloha Hawaiian Airlines. We had a load of baggage, but all went well. We stayed at the *Maui Sun* last night. It was a nice hotel off the beach on the lower west coast.

Today we moved to the upper west coast to the *Ka'anapali Beach Hotel.* This is my second time at this hotel. It is a really friendly place in a very convenient location. We have a room with a great view of the pool and the grounds and our balcony overlooks the ocean. There is a great beach. We walked along the beachfront over to the *Whaler.* There they had a fantastic group playing jazz with a wonderful, energetic black woman singing up a storm. She sounded like my old favorite jazz singer, Sarah Vaughan.

Her name is Kelly Covington. She is well known for her singing and for her jazz group. She not only sang great but when she wasn't singing she was a ball of energy inspiring the other musicians with her enthusiasm. She reminded me of a great jazz trumpeter named Maynard Ferguson who I'd seen about a year ago. Maynard Ferguson must be my age or older and he is famous for his screeching high register trumpet solos. Perhaps you would remember his recording of the theme from the movie *Rocky.*

Ferguson had a young powerful band that really soared. He has a wild head of white hair. When he isn't playing himself, he stands in front of the band waving out the beat and exhorting the young musicians as they solo. At the end of each solo he would call out the soloists name and lead the applause.

When he played duets with his young musicians, he directed all of the applause to the others, taking none for himself. Then he would embrace the musicians, shaking their hands in congratulations. If ever there was a visible sign of management by coaching and cheerleading this was it.

It was so obvious that his band members loved him and their solos were absolutely magnificent. The enthusiastic way he treated them drove them to new levels of excellence. This elevated Ferguson to higher levels of performance himself. He was staying young and vital by helping to bring out the greatness in others.

We enjoyed the wonderful jazz on the beach for a while, then we walked on. Hawaii is hard to describe. I find myself tempted to pull out a travel brochure in a hope to find adequate words to describe this endless beauty. We were driving between hotels today and the beauty was so great that we pulled over to drink it in. Terry could not resist the scene and soon he had his video camera out shooting scenes of waves, surfers and boats. Then the scene overcame me too and we were soon shooting a short video on catching the wave.

It reminded me how many of us say we will do something as soon as.. "Just as soon as I finish high school." "Just as soon as I finish college." Or maybe, "As soon as I get a good job." Maybe, "After I get married or after the kids are grown." Here is another, "When we get the children through college." The good waves, the opportunities for travel, for adventure, for a business of our own, for many of these things that make life a joy and a blessing pass us by. Then perhaps it is "As soon as you get your health back, dear."

Then one day you realize all of the waves, all the opportunities have gone. Then you sit and play that, "should have, could have, would have" game. Today is the time for action. Why not join me? Let's go for the wave now.

One Way Bridge

*I*n our walk yesterday we visited the *Whalers Village*. It is a modern shopping center built on the site of an old fishing village where the whalers used to live when they weren't out chasing whales.

They have a wonderful exhibit out on the mall. There is an absolutely breathtaking gold and silver sculpture of an eagle swooping down to catch a huge fish. It is the work of artist Chester Field and it is titled *Splashdown*.

Early this morning, Terry and I were back at *Whaler's Village* with his camera. Soon the camera was rolling. I began telling the story of the baby eagle whose parents were killed and how it was raised with a farmer's chickens.

As I told the story, I looked up at the magnificent sculpture of the eagle. "It might have been this very eagle." I said. "How are we to know this eagle's background?" I asked. Terry shot me from a bridge at the mall, then he moved his camera and shot it again.

He wasn't satisfied with the background, so he went down off the bridge to an area below. Then we did it again. This time all he had in the picture was the eagle, myself and a beautiful blue Hawaiian sky in the background.

"I've got it!" Terry finally called out to me. "I've got it and it is great." I don't know how the video came out as yet, but I had to agree with him. I am an eagle nut. I love eagles and that sculpture *Splashdown* by Chester Fields is more than great. It is the most beautiful eagle I have ever seen. A bit later we started out to further explore Maui.

I must have driven around two thousand sharp curves, and over five dozen one lane bridges today. The views were absolutely awesome. We visited the rain forest where we made a great video. Later we pulled over and saw yet another view that my poor vocabulary simply cannot do justice to.

Maui is too much of a challenge to me when it comes to the right words for an adequate description. I can see a visitor from the flatlands being rushed to a Maui hospital and after careful examination the physician would say, "This poor fellow overdosed on grandeur."

We pulled off the road and watched the sun sink into the Pacific. My heart is simply overflowing with the beauty that is Maui and its people. As the sun went out of view I said a silent prayer of thanks for our being here to witness it.

Volcano

*I*ncredible! I saved that word for today. Utterly incredible. Watching dawn atop the *Haleakala Volcano*. The phone rang at 2:15 A.M. in our room. Terry leaped for the phone and responded with a bright, cheery "Good morning."

The van from *Maui Mountain Cruisers* driven by a young man named Wolf arrived shortly after 2:45 A.M. The van was already full when we got in and then two more squeezed in with us. We made a stop at their headquarters and picked up a trailer with the bikes and a ride guide named Greg.

We had three young Japanese girls from Tokyo who giggled through the entire trip. They were a joy to be with. Enroute, the full moon glowed on the incoming waves. It was magnificent. We drove the thirty-eight miles uphill in time to see the first red glow of the approaching dawn. As we pulled into the parking lot we saw dozens of other cars and vans.

There were a couple of hundred people at the summit gathered to watch the sunrise. We donned warm pants and jackets, then added warm gloves. Many of the other folks wrapped themselves in blankets because it was about forty degrees above zero at the top.

We watched the sky which was clear above us. Out beyond the crater there were huge clouds below us. At 6:00 A.M. the sky was brilliant as the sun came up above a cloud. It was actually a spiritual experience for me. There was an eerie sense of being up there at the summit with the new day.

Personally I thought about my own bright new future starting this day at exactly 6:00 A.M. My life seemed to have a bright new meaning. I made a silent promise to make a greater effort to do something of significance in the very near future.

Then once the dawn was up we were assigned our cruising bikes for a bike ride I will never forget. Imagine, me riding a bike for thirty-eight miles. That's right, I made that trip like a young kid. Of course, it was all down hill. We had these huge helmets, plus really caring guides who took extra time to give us the careful training so we could make the trip safely.

The scenery was really different with horses, and cows who appeared to have a strange looking bird assigned to them. I felt like a million bucks, at least when I completed that trip. Most of the people with us were in their twenties. Terry is a seasoned biker who bikes several thousand miles each year. I ride around the block on my relic bike at least twice a year; so there was a special thrill for me when I made it the entire thirty-eight miles without the slightest problem.

Again, I thank God for those walks around the mall getting ready for this dream trip. It is shortly after 3:00 P.M., and time for my nap now. I think I earned it. Every foot of this island and its surroundings holds a new adventure for us. What a splendid world this is. Yes, we know better than ever that God's beauty is all around us.

In the early evening we drove down to Lahaina and met Earl and Margo Watkins. Earl is an expert camera person at Channel 7 Television in Detroit working with Terry. Margo is a successful freelance writer. We had a really enjoyable visit. Then as Terry and I walked along Front Street we looked at the ocean and noticed the sun was about to set into some low flying clouds at the horizon.

We stood there spellbound as the sun went down. We'd seen it rise on the summit and now we watched it as it slowly sank into the Pacific. This is our last evening on Maui. I swear I am overdosed on awesome beauty. I'll sleep soundly tonight and pray that Terry has not arranged another 2:15 A.M. wake up.

Aloha!

A half hour at the beach and who do I run into but five women from Michigan. One worked for Mazda and on an impulse I gave her my card. Terry and I have been packing this morning. We have a bit of shopping to do. Terry wants to wrap all of the videos in aluminum foil to avoid possible x-ray damage by the airlines, and so we made a quick trip to *Whaler's Village*.

I had a friend I wanted to visit on Maui who ran a shop called *The Pearl Connection*. His name is Tim Hackbarth and he is a musician. Ruthie and I visited his shop on our trip two years before and Ruthie found some wonderful pearls.

I discovered that Tim had a band and I arranged for him to record a song I had written titled *Downsizen*. They did a great job and now before our afternoon flight we had rediscovered Tim's shop. Terry and I did our last minute shopping at Tim's shop and at a shirt store next door.

When I walked into Tim's store he looked at me and tried to remember me. I solved his problem by singing a few bars of my song..

There's guys in suits from IBM and truckers here, galore.
A ton of folks from old GM & soon there will be more.
There's lots of those mid-managers and common folks here too.
But with foreign competition it seemed the thing to do.

Art Fettig (c) 1992

His face brightened and he called out, "Art." and embraced me. When you make a purchase at *The Pearl Connection*, Tim leads you over to a little counter where he lets you pick out a free bonus. I took a little pair of earrings this time, and I took a warm feeling too. Gee it is great to find an old friend and renew an acquaintance, even if it was just a brief encounter of a couple of years ago.

After that Terry and I went out and shot some video of wind surfers and some stuff on sugar cane mills. We were pretty well on schedule when Terry discovered he had lost his glasses, perhaps in a sugar cane field. He went back while I staked out a restaurant. When he returned he was without his glasses.

We grabbed a quick bite and headed for the airport. The line was absolutely impossible and we ended up tipping a sky cap $10. It was the smallest bill I had and I was so glad to be rid of those heavy bags. We went directly to the departure gate, found a dozen in line and a computer that was down.

We had some anxious moments, but they finally wrote some magic numbers on our tickets. We were almost the last to board. With stress and baggage to carry we were both sopping wet with sweat, really ready for a shower. If we fly on time then Detroit is only nine hours away. We have a stop off in Chicago, but we don't have to change planes.

I plan to end this little book with our landing in Detroit. Terry and I are still speaking to one another. I am still in awe of his talents. One thing I learned though is that we are the real odd couple.

Perhaps you remember the television show, *The Odd Couple*, featuring Tony Randall and Jack Klugman. Felix and Oscar. In the television show, Felix was a photographer; Terry is a photographer using his television camera. Oscar was a writer. I write. Felix was neat and tidy; so is Terry. I am afraid I am a bit of a slob. Quite a bit.

I won't go into detail; let's just say we are very different. I hope it didn't get in our way. I enjoyed this trip from the very moment it began. I believe Terry feels that way too. It was the best vacation I've ever had, if you'd care to call it a vacation. As far as I can tell we worked every day, either shooting video, giving speeches, exhibiting or doing research. It has been a fabulous *Showtime.*

I asked Terry what was the best event or moment of all. Without hesitation he said, "The sunrise and the downhill bike ride." I might agree with him, but for me, reaching the top of *Diamond Head* was really meaningful. It made me feel that life was good and rewarding.

I was able to pull my belt in a full three notches this morning. I feel absolutely wonderful. My high hopes are soaring in the clouds. We've had some wonderful invitations to return to Hawaii for both speeches and seminars, as well as video projects. We've had invites to Alaska, California, Louisiana, Illinois and even an invite to speak in Battle Creek.

Life goes on. It is good and I know better now than I have ever known that this is truly a beautiful world filled with exciting, loving, caring people.

Terry is anxious to get on with setting up his new video editing equipment to work on editing our tapes. Me? I'm anxious to get back to my regular routine. There are new speeches to book, new audiences to entertain and inspire. I've got a whole new life to get on with. Today is the first day of the rest of my life, so let's get on with it.

It's Showtime.

Afterward

When I subtitled this book "How To Make Thousands Vacationing in Hawaii" I really did not want to mislead anyone. Terry and I made literally, thousands of new friends. We both plan to return to Hawaii in the near future for more work, more play and more great fellowship with the new friends we've both made there.

We managed to pay for all our travel expenses and still come out a few thousand dollars ahead. Then we have our video tapes, our precious, wonderful video tapes. No doubt they will prove to be revenue producing too.

More than friends or dollars though we have our precious memories. Some of our friends try to hassle us about the fact that we both work on our vacations. Actually, unfortunately, they do not understand that what we do is not work at all. If it is labor, then it is definitely a labor of love. Speaking for me is a passion and that is the way Terry feels about creating video productions.

For us, at times, life is just one huge, joyous, exciting adventure. Call it work, call it play, call it what you will, we thrive on it and look forward to our next challenge. Somewhere, very soon, it will be

Showtime

About the Author

Art Fettig was born in Detroit, Michigan July 5, 1929. In 1960 he moved his family to Battle Creek, Michigan, where he now resides. He married Ruthie, his wife of over thirty-eight years and she died of cancer, June 26, 1993. They have four grown children and four grandchildren.

Art Fettig began writing professionally in 1961 and he has had thirty-two books published, including *How To Hold An Audience In The Hollow Of Your Hand, The Three Robots* series of children's stories, *The Platinum Rule, Love Is The Target* and *Serenity! Serenity!*

In 1963 he began his career as a professional speaker and has made presentations in all fifty of the United States, eight Canadian Provinces and several other foreign locations including Malaysia and Hong Kong. He is now the veteran of well over 3,000 professional presentations.

Today, Art Fettig spends a great deal of time writing and making presentations in the Safety Field. His current client list includes such firms as General Motors, DuPont, Exxon, Akzo and major safety conferences and conventions throughout the world.

In 1980 he was certified as a "Speaking Professional" (C.S.P.) by the National Speakers Association. Art continues to write and lecture on personal growth, motivation and sales. He is a frequent visitor to elementary schools where he speaks for students on "Saying yes to positive living."

Art Fettig is featured in a number of video programs on safety, and on several cassette tape programs.

During the Korean Conflict, Fettig served as a combat rifleman in the United States Army. He was wounded in combat and was awarded *The Military Order of the Purple Heart.*

For information on his availability as a professional speaker, or for a free catalog of his books and audio-visual products, please contact Art Fettig's Growth Unlimited Inc., 36 Fairview, Battle Creek, Michigan 49017. Phone (800) 441-7676 or (616) 965-2229. The Fax number is (616) 965-4522.

Art Fettig's Inspirational Products
Books and Tapes That May Touch Your Life

Platinum Rule

The powerful secret to attaining great wealth
and happiness. Thousands sold by word of mouth.

Paperback Edition $5.95
Audio Tape $9.95
Hardcover Autographed Edition $12.95

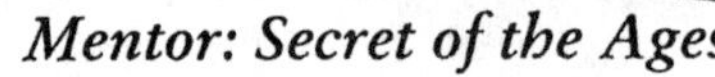

Mentor: Secret of the Ages

You will be introduced to your own personal
"mentor," your "friend in need" in time of crisis.
Whenever you want you'll be able to turn to this
written masterpiece for guidance and comfort.

Hardcover Autographed Edition $9.95
Paperback edition $5.95
Audio Tape $9.95

Serenity! Serenity! Living the Serenity Prayer

One man's quest for serenity, acceptance and courage.
A must for those in recovery or anyone seeking joy.
Paperback $5.95

Love is the Target
An Answer for Troubled Americans Today

This little book will provide you with
the answer you seek to live a happier,
healthier, more productive life.

Paperback $5.95

Now Available on Audio and Video Tapes

This funny, fun and inspirational presentation captures
all of the joy and high energy of a live performance.

Love is the Target Video $39.95
Audio Tape $9.95

Special-Get All Three!
The book, the audio and the video for just $40.00

Attention Professional Speakers and Toastmasters

Three All New Videos Created Especially for Speakers

See Art Fettig live in the comfort of your own home or listen to him on tape in your car.

In Hawaii Art Fettig made 3 incredible videos just for speakers. Let an expert show you how it is really done on these sensational videos.

Becoming a Professional Speaker Art Fettig speaks for members of the Hawaiian Chapter of the National Speakers Association about turning a part-time writing hobby into a full-time speaking career.

From Toastmasters to Rain Forests on Maui A personal session on speaking with Art Fettig, in the rain forest on Maui. How to build a professional speech 5 to 7 minutes at a time.

Making $2,000 to $20,000 a Day (By Using Your Talents) Another one to one session with Art Fettig on money, commitment and success.

Videos
$39.95 each or buy all 3 for $95.00

SAVE $69.90 Buy all three videos and the Speaker's Kit for just $110.00

Call Today
800 441-7676

Art of Public Speaking Kit

Get the *Art of Public Speaking* 6 audio tape cassette album and *How to Hold an Audience in the Hollow of Your Hand* book, *Anatomy of a Speech Booklet* and the *Humor Game* book. This book/tape package will immediately increase your impact on every audience you face. Make speech preparation easier and more fun. *$59.95*

Buy the book "How To Hold An Audience In The Hollow Of Your Hand" <u>ONLY $9.95</u>

All New Videos for Teachers

NEW The Powerful New *Declaration of Inter-Dependence* Video for Educators

In this entertaining, inspirational 9 tape series, Art Fettig adds sparkle to your in-service meetings. More important, he will help renew the commitment and dedication of every teacher. This series features the *Declaration of Inter-Dependence for Educators*, plus 8 short meeting sizzlers.

* *A Declaration of Inter-Dependence for Educators 24 Minutes*
* *The Wisdom of the World's Greatest Philosophers 7 Minutes*
* *Enthusiastic Arithmetic 6 Minutes*
* *Bringing Out That Music In You 10 Minutes*
* *Teacher, Teacher, We Love You 10 Minutes*
* *Circles, Squares, Triangles and Squiggley Lines 5 Minutes*
* *The Great Teachers in Your Life 11 Minutes*
* *We've Got To Be Taught To Love 8 Minutes*
* *Growth-A Daily Challenge 7 Minutes*

Just $495 or call for individual prices

Win personal commitment from your entire staff with this proven series

Call Us Today at 800 441-7676

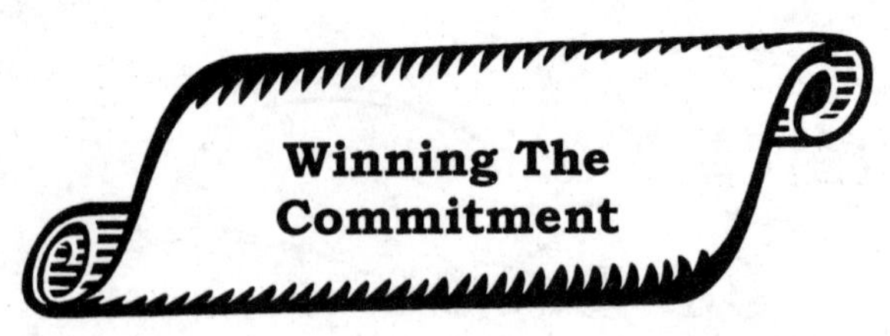

By far the highlight of the Hawaii trip was the presentations given for the Safety Engineers and the Governor's Pacific Rim Conference. See these dramatic, live performances on video. *Winning a Commitment to Safety* includes a powerful story about Captain James Cook of the British Navy and his solution to the unnecessary deaths caused by scurvy and other diseases. In the talk for Safety Engineers, *Developing a Passion for Safety*, Art talks about the movie *Schlinder's List*, and gives a special challenge to safety people. *Only $59.95 each*

> **You'll gain a greater knowledge of what a commitment and passion for safety are all about and how it affects each of us at work and at home. Don't miss out. Call today for more information on these new videos. 800-441-7676**

A **Must** for everyone in the Safety Field.

Also Available on Video

The Declaration of Inter-Dependence for Safety, taped live with an audience of blue collar workers, this inspiring presentation contains the signing of the *Declaration for Safety* and a commitment to positive inter-action. Show it to your employees now and win their support. *34 minutes*

$295

Call Today 800 441-7676

Follow Through Every Month With

The Best of Art Fettig
Video Series

Did you ever wish you had a special bit of video to set the mood for a meeting, something powerful and emotional to close with? Maybe you need a little lift yourself, or maybe you'd like to study Fettig's professional speaking style.

Art Fettig has been a published author for over thirty years and a professional speaker for over twenty. He has created literally hundreds of hours of special speech material. Many top professional speakers consider his work the best in the business.

Both Earl Nightingale and Paul Harvey have used his material in their radio shows. Dozens of the world's top professional speakers, including Art Linkletter, Cavett Robert and Herb True, Ph.D. use his material in their speeches.

This is a continuing video series with new offerings from work in progress. Now you can enhance your meetings with these powerful segments, you'll find a number of uses for meetings, conventions and training sessions. Give your meetings a lift. Each video contains four different segments.

The Best of Art Fettig

Volume 1

Schindler's List *(3:18 Minutes) From a live presentation to American Navy personnel at Pearl Harbor in Hawaii, these dramatic presentations demonstrate and encourage compassion to our fellow human beings.*

The Song Inside *(10:47 Minutes) Recorded at a teacher in-service seminar, this segment demonstrates to the audience how they can be a sounding board for every student or fellow individual they touch.*

Old Violin *(2:42) Minutes Fettig renders the classic verse, <u>The Touch of the Master's Hand.</u>*

Volume 2

The Power of One *(5:30 Minutes) How one woman's effort changed the environment of thousands.*

Original Has This Signature *(4:53 Minutes) Visiting W.K. Kellogg's home and talking about quality.*

Teacher, Teacher, We Love You *(6:02 Minutes) Recorded at a teacher in-service seminar, Art show how teachers are appreciated through Art's "Here's Johnny Segment" along with a reading of his poem, <u>Teacher, Teacher, We Love You.</u>*

Fly With The Eagles *(2:44 Minutes) During one of the thousands of presentations that Art has done, a recent trip to Hawaii drew him to the Island of Maui and a gallery featuring the sculptures of Chester Fields. A tale about excellence.*

Volume 3

Somebody Threw A Bottle *(2:49 minutes) Art Fettig on the railroad tracks near his home in Battle Creek reflecting on his poem, <u>Somebody Threw A Bottle</u>. Tragedy strikes the railroad resulting in a needless death.*

Volunteers *(8:30 Minutes) A gentle winter walk through a snow covered park along a flowing brook glimmering with ice. Art reflects on his volunteering and how it has affected his life.*

My Brother Joe *(6:07 Minutes) A talk about Vietnam and alcohol. A moving tribute to veteran's. Powerful!*

Interacting To Communicate *(3:11 minutes) A cup, a pitcher of water and a thirst come together to demonstrate in a very humorous way that knowledge without interaction simply becomes a waste. This segment is from a presentation to military personnel in Hawaii.*

Order these marvelous videos today and enhance your meetings!

Make your programs sparkle!

Humor! Motivation! Inspiration!

Just $59.95 each or all 3 for just $140.00

Call Art Today To Order
(800) 441-7676

Art Fettig's
Growth Unlimited Inc.
Dedicated to bringing positive living concepts to people.
36 Fairview Battle Creek, Michigan 49017
(616) 965-2229 or (800) 441-7676 Fax (616) 965-4522

Item No.	Description	Quantity	Price Each	Price Total
			Subtotal	
			MI Res, 4% Tax	
			+ 10% Shipping ($3 Minimum)	

Please find my check or money order enclosed | **Total Order** |

Charge my VISA ❏ **MasterCard** ❏ **or American Express** ❏

Card No: ______________________ Expires (Mo/Yr): ______________

Signature: ____________________ Tel. No: ______________________

Name: ____

Address: ____

City: ________________ St: ____________ Zip: ________________

We guarantee 100% satisfaction on all of our products. If, for any reason, you are not delighted with any of our products, just return them for a 100% refund.

SEND IN YOUR ORDER TODAY!